THE
SOUND
OF
JAZZ

THE SOUND OF JAZZ

JOHN FORDHAM

GALLERY BOOKS
An Imprint of W. H. Smith Publishers Inc.
112 Madison Avenue
New York City 10016

Photographic Acknowledgments
The Bettmann Archive, Inc. 68–9; BBC Hulton Picture
Library 14–15, 17 top; Dat's Jazz Picture Library 136; Frank
Driggs Collection 12, 13, 34, 45 left, 47 top, 53, 72 top, 77
bottom, 82, 91, 108 top, 109 bottom, 121, 137 bottom, 141,
145, 148 bottom, (Joe Alper) 86; Jak Kilby 24 top, 49 top
right and bottom, 60, 75 bottom, 88, 130–1, 135, 144
bottom; Jean-Pierre Leloir 101; London Features International
Ltd/Steve Rapport 30–31; Octopus Publishing Group 16
bottom, 36 right, 52, 92 bottom; Pictorial Press Ltd 16 top,
35; David Redfern Photography 4–5, 10, 22 left, 22–3, 24
bottom, 25 top and bottom, 26, 27 right, 28 left, 28–9, 30
left, 31 top, 32, 36 left, 38, 39 left and right, 40 top and
bottom, 41, 42, 46, 47 bottom, 48, 50, 54–5, 56–7, 58–9, 59,
63, 64–5, 65 top, 66, 69, 70–71 top, 73, 74, 75 top, 76
bottom, 76–7 top, 78, 79 top and bottom, 83, 84, 85, 87 left
and right, 90, 92–3 top, 95 top and bottom, 96–7, 98, 99 top
and bottom, 100, 102–103 bottom, 103 top, 104, 105, 108
bottom, 109 top, 110, 115, 118, 119, 122 top and bottom,
124–5, 126, 128–9, 131 bottom, 132, 133, 134, 138, 139 top,
140–41, 142, 143 top and bottom, 146, 148 top, 149, 150,
151, 152–3, 153 top right, (Dave Ellis) 70 bottom left,
(William Gottlieb) 17 bottom, 18, 19, 20, 21, 37, 44, 45 top
and bottom right, 70 bottom right, 72 bottom, 80, 94, 102
top, 106, 112–13, 114, 116, (Andrew Putler) 61, 144 top,
(Schapowalow) 127, (Chuch Stewart) 128; Nico van der
Stam 27 left; Camilla van Zuylen 40 top left.

First published in 1989 by
The Hamlyn Publishing Group Limited
a division of
The Octopus Publishing Group
Michelin House
81 Fulham Road
London SW3 6RB

This edition published in 1989 by Gallery Books
An imprint of W H Smith Publishers Inc
W H Smith Publishers Inc
112 Madison Avenue
New York, New York 10016

Copyright © The Hamlyn Publishing Group Limited 1989
First published in 1989
ISBN 0-8317-78970

Produced by Mandarin Offset
Printed and bound in Hong Kong

CONTENTS

ABOVE *Louis Armstrong*

RIGHT *Charlie Parker*

INTRODUCTION

Clint Eastwood recently forgot his normally noncommital style sufficiently to observe the contribution of the United States to the cultural life of humankind had been the Western and jazz music. The occasion for this eloquence was the launch of Eastwood's film *Bird*, about the life and times of Charlie Parker. Whatever you may think about either the Western or jazz, the making of such a mainstream film in 1988 demonstrates that jazz is currently passing through one of its periods of popularity. With enthusiastic young fans discovering the music for the first time, and possibly enthusiastic older ones rekindling the old passion for it, there seemed a need for a book that attempted to fill in some of the historical background, and at the same time set itself the slippery but attractive task of trying to capture the *sound* of jazz on paper.

Words and pictures are, of course, no substitute for experiencing this fiery, impulsive and soulful music at first hand. But since many of the music's most eminent pioneers have now passed on, and the understandable urge of young players to issue repro versions of past triumphs appears to be accelerating, it is perhaps desirable that at least a working knowledge of jazz history should be more common among music-lovers than it is today. It is also hoped that *The Sound of Jazz* may tempt the reader into nooks and crannies of the music's rich seam that might not otherwise have been explored.

Inevitably, constraints of space have made their demands on the scope of this book. There has not been space for extensive discographies, but these days the specialist jazz record shops nearly always go out of their way to be helpful, and there are many specialized books to which you can refer. There has also not been room for the full procession of talent that might have marched past in a treatment of how the sound of jazz developed. Though the music could not have happened outside of its particular history – most notably the aftermath of the slave trade to the United States and the often difficult lives of black people in American cities – it is also quintessentially a music of individuals. All jazz players strive to find a sound instantly recognizable as theirs. For this reason, a survey of the changing sound of the music through its relatively short life could easily deal with the contributions of many hundreds of players and we have had to content ourselves with a selection.

But if you came to love jazz, and its free spirit, then you can easily spend a lifetime marvelling at its infinite variety. If the sound of jazz – or, as the great American commentator Whitney Balliett put it, 'the sound of surprise' – really gets to you, many of those names that didn't make it on to these pages will become close friends soon enough.

John Fordham
London, April 1989

CHAPTER ONE

FROM
RAGS
TO
RICHES

❛ The history of jazz can be
told in four words:
Louis Armstrong, Charlie Parker ❜

MILES DAVIS

The death of the ragtime pianist Eubie Blake in 1983 was a reminder that the history of jazz is only now passing beyond the point at which it could be encompassed by a single lifetime. In the space of less than a century, jazz has passed from folk-art to avant-garde. All of its ports of call along that route are still strongly discernible today, both in the work of surviving originals, and in younger players who have adapted and celebrated the triumphs of the past. It is

Modern jazz genius, Charlie 'Bird' Parker. The New York graffiti defiantly declared 'Bird Lives' after his death in 1955. His musical influence has been incalculable, inside and outside jazz.

the life-blood of virtually all Western popular music, and is beginning to influence musics of the wider world, and to be influenced by them in its turn.

Jazz music does not solely contain African elements, but if African culture had not mingled – even under the conditions of slavery – with European musical forms, there would have been no jazz in the way that we conceive of it today. Without Africa, the sounds that give jazz its most intense and characteristic life would have been absent. Most West African traditional music gives rhythmic variation the central role that European music gives to melody. African suites would thus take the form of a succession of different rhythmic patterns rather than contrasting constructions in pitch. But the music of the continent did not reject melody; it merely reversed its significance.

In West Africa, as in the folk musics of civilizations as dispersed as those of the Celts, American Indians, Chinese and Mexicans, the scales in use were pentatonic – they used five notes, with no semitones, or half-steps. The European diatonic scale (the do-re-me scale of primary schools) has seven notes, consisting of five whole steps and two half-steps.

Traditional African singers had trouble with the diatonic scale, which they became acquainted with when European missionaries tried to teach them hymns. The attempts of vocalists raised on a five-note scale to sing the additional ones – and their efforts to wriggle out of it or turn the unfamiliar elements back into their own vocabulary by bending or slurring the sounds – is generally taken to be the origin of the 'blue' or oddly flattened tones so characteristic of jazz.

African musical traditions were also quite different in relation to time. African patterns strongly feature a 'ternary' time – three notes or a triplet over a single beat. European metres, particularly for hymns, were based on duple time – two notes to a beat. Mixtures of duple and triple time are at the heart of African music, and subsequently they became the complex heartbeat of jazz.

As the slaves in North America began to absorb their surroundings, and looked for means of protesting their plight and making its tribulations pass more easily, two new scales emerged from the old roots. One was the spiritual or 'shout scale' – a modified pentatonic. The other was the blue scale, with the third and seventh notes flattened – though not by a full half-step; the exact pitch would be hard to measure as it constantly varied. With these new sounds came blues. And with the cross-rhythms of the African continent came ragtime.

New Orleans was not the only place in which the alchemy that led to jazz was happening. But some accidents of circumstance led to it becoming the most significant. Located at the mouth of the Mississippi–Missouri river system (which made it an obvious target in the struggle for European supremacy over America), it was a town of itinerants and immigrants. Its population included whites, blacks in slavery until the Civil War, and 'free persons of colour'. The 'free Negroes' or 'Creoles' had won their freedom during the period of French colonialism.

Creole education always featured training in European classical music. But it would be blended into a musical repertoire that included contemporary popular songs, music from operettas and from dance. New Orleans was the first American city to have regular opera, and since the opera houses were divided into separate sections for freed blacks and slaves, there was a substantial black attendance.

One musical outcome of this diversity of black culture in the South was ragtime. Its most celebrated practitioner was Scott Joplin, a Texan who settled in Sedalia, Missouri, in the last decade of the 19th century. The name of the music he played was taken from the merger of European music – drawn from Chopin and Liszt – with a curious rhythmic shift into, literally, 'ragged time'. The style was rhythmic,

open, inviting, accessible. It took off in the railheads and overnight boom towns around Sedalia, Kansas, St. Louis and in Texas. Piano players delivered it in saloons across the States, and where there weren't piano players there were piano rolls, the spiked cylinders that activated automatic player-pianos. 'The Entertainer', 'Solace' and 'Maple Leaf Rag' were all enduring songs from Joplin's pen.

Syncopated rhythm broke the European rules. In orthodox triple-time music the second and third beats of a bar were normally unaccented. In ragtime, the pianist's two hands would be placing a contrasting rhythm – accents placed on the normally 'quiet' beats by the right hand playing the treble part, while the conventional accenting goes on in the left. European music had used the idea before, but only as an effect. For their harmonies, the ragtime musicians borrowed the construction of chords more usually deployed by banjo players, as well as many of the sound effects of brass band music like John Philip Souza's.

Joplin was the master. He composed more than 600 rags and two operas, and his work bridged the divide between European art-music and black folk-music. Along with Tom Turpin, James Scott, Louis Chauvin and Eubie Blake, Joplin laid the foundation stone for a craze, and one which later came to be mutated into a part, but a vital part, of what came to be called 'jazz'. But this music was not improvised; it

was written. Jelly Roll Morton, a New Orleans musician of great imagination, was one of the first to add spontaneous variations to ragtime compositions. The skill even led Morton to claim parenthood of ragtime itself.

There was another vital strand. In the countryside, black slaves sang work songs in the plantations and spirituals in the open air as new converts to Christianity. But from the middle of the 19th century there had also been a rural music with distinct similarities to the blues, though at that time lacking its characteristic bar structure and beat.

In the late 19th century New Orleans boomed, and it became the South's biggest port. This status unsurprisingly produced Storyville, a teeming red-light district, established by a city ordinance in 1898 formulated by Alderman Sidney Story. And in Storyville demands for music, and opportunities for a new kind of music, grew more powerful than ever.

Musicians in New Orleans now had plenty of outlets. They could play in the bordellos of Storyville at night; they could play for local dances; they could play at festivals and on parades. The instruments

LEFT *Scott Joplin, the king of 'ragged time'. Ragtime involved almost no improvising, but rhythmically it paved the way for jazz.*

BELOW *A famous picture of the Buddy Bolden Band, circa 1895. Bolden (standing, with cornet) had a chequered career that preceded recording, so his work lives on only as legend.*

were an alfresco blend of the Creole favourite – the clarinet – with the staples of marching bands and military bands. The annual Mardi Gras festival was a sensational testimony to the significance of dance and music in the town's everyday life. And the French and Italian custom of playing a dirge to take departed ones to the cemetery and party music to usher the procession back home survived to be performed by the New Orleans jazz bands.

The availability of instruments took a sudden upturn with the conclusion of the Spanish-American war in 1898, since New Orleans was one of the closest ports to the action. When the soldiers came home and the units were demobbed, the military bands broke up with them. As a result, in 1900, the junk shops of New Orleans were overflowing with cheap musical instruments. There were plenty of clarinets and drums. There were also plenty of trombones and cornets. Even poor black citizens of the town could afford to buy an instrument.

The characteristic sound of an early New Orleans band was the counterpoint, or intertwining of three melodic lines – usually from a trumpet or cornet, a trombone and a clarinet. The impact of the cornet is bright, glowing, assertive. The trombone underpins it with broad, sweeping sounds, like a large paintbrush being smeared across a canvas. Like a dancer, the clarinet weaves balletically between the two. The rhythms were not yet the rhythms that became the trademark of jazz. They were the beat of street marches and the circus bands, or of the ensembles that toured the city on carts – 'band-wagons'. Syncopation, so far appropriated by rag-time, was yet to join the New Orleans musicians' party.

Considering the extent of the advantage conferred by being white in turn-of-the-century America, it wasn't surprising that the first successful jazz bands out of the South should have been white. The father of them was Papa Jack Laine, who ran a band in New Orleans from 1891. Laine hired a trumpeter called Nick LaRocca in the 1910s, a strong player who was nonetheless self-taught and couldn't read music. LaRocca eventually found himself in a 'hot' band featuring drummer Johnny Stein, and it was this outfit that was heard by a visiting Chicagoan, who arranged for them to play a season in a Chicago nightclub. Stein left and the name became the Original Dixieland Jass Band.

A booking followed in early 1917 at New York's Reisenweber's Restaurant. Close on the heels of their smash hit appearance there, the band went into the Victor Studios in New York on 26 February 1917 to cut the first jazz record (featuring the tunes 'Livery Stable Blues' and 'Dixieland Jass Band One-Step'). The work of that day took a music that had hitherto been played – as James Lincoln Collier put it – by 'a

few hundred blacks and a handful of whites in New Orleans and rarely heard elsewhere', and turned it into a world-wide craze. The word 'jazz' is reputed to have appeared in a San Francisco newspaper as early as 1913. But the words 'jass', 'jasm' and 'gism' – all with sexual connotations – had been in use a long while before that.

Though there were, from before the turn of the century, black New Orleans bands led by trumpeters like Buddy Bolden, Bunk Johnson and Freddie Keppard playing a kind of pre-jazz (some of the Afro-American intonation but with marching or street-parade rhythms), the first decisive step into a completely new idiom that altered melody, harmony and rhythm, was taken by King Oliver's Creole Jazz Band. Joseph 'King' Oliver was born in 1885 and began playing with a local brass band as a teenager. By 1910 he was good enough to get regular work, became a familiar figure around Storyville, and was regarded eventually as one of the foremost jazz musicians in the locality.

14

King Oliver's Creole Jazz Band in the early 1920s. The band was a foundation stone of the New Orleans movement, and it launched the career of the first jazz genius, Louis Armstrong (at the centre on trumpet). Lil Hardin Armstrong is on piano.

The overnight success of the Original Dixieland band provided the impetus for Oliver's reputation to spread further afield. In early 1918 Oliver went to Chicago and played regularly around the city over the next couple of years. In 1922, Oliver got his chance to lead his own band. He called it King Oliver's Creole Jazz Band. It featured Johnny Dodds on clarinet, Baby Dodds on drums, Honore Dutrey on trombone, Lil Hardin on piano and Bill Johnson on bass. Not long afterwards, Oliver invited a young man called Louis Armstrong to share the front-line duties with him. In 1923 the band recorded. Indistinct and difficult to listen to though these records are, they are the first recorded examples of true jazz.

The characteristics that marked out this music were polyphony (several melodies playing at the same time); the strict division of responsibilities so that Oliver would play the lead line based on the melody while Armstrong varied it or harmonized it, with Dodds and Dutrey linking the melodic statements; and a far more sophisticated structure than formerly, with tunes including main themes and subsidiaries. The 'rough' inflections of jazz, however – so significantly absent from the O.D.J.B. – are clearly audible.

The groundwork was done; the music only needed a revolutionary leader. Louis Armstrong was that inspiration. He was born on 4 July 1900. His grandparents had been slaves, his father was a labourer and his mother a domestic and part-time prostitute, but the boy was raised in the New Orleans ghetto by his grandmother, Josephine. Despite poverty, and the daily proximity to drunkenness, vice, drugs, crime and sudden death, the young Armstrong became a cheerful, resourceful and robust teenager.

On New Year's Day 1913 the young Armstrong's enthusiasm so ran away with him that he fired a live revolver in the street to let off steam. This offence took him into the Colored Waifs' Home, and Armstrong's more formal musical education began. He joined the school's brass band, first on tambourine, then on drums, then on alto horn. Though the 14-year-old had already revealed an uncanny sense of time on the percussion instruments, it was his ability – with no musical education at all – to improvise a harmonic counterpart to what the other instruments were doing that marked him out as something very special. He became the Waifs' Home's bugler, he then learned the cornet, and thereafter became leader of the band.

As his cornet playing progressed, Armstrong began to secure more of the regular New Orleans and Storyville gigs. He met King Oliver through trombonist Kid Ory's cabaret band, and the older trumpeter probably showed him how the staples of the New Orleans bandbook were played.

At the beginning of the 1920s there began a great exodus of New Orleans entertainers to Chicago. Storyville had been closed down by the navy when New Orleans devoted its energies to assisting in the European war effort. The loss of income drove the locality's various professionals north. In that period Louis Armstrong had hovered between riverboat jobs (a fellow musician on the boats gave him some rudimentary lessons in reading the dots) and the regular New Orleans outlets, before Oliver summoned him to Chicago. This was Armstrong's big break, and the young trumpeter stayed with his mentor for two years.

On the early records, Oliver unquestionably demonstrates the true jazz musician's facility for gaining the maximum of expressiveness from the leanest of raw materials. But Armstrong had a burning tone in all registers and a composer's feel for logical and balanced statements. Above all, he had a rhythmic audacity that left his improvisations hanging on the beat by an elastic bond that could be endlessly stretched but snapped him back to the heart of a song when it counted. More than anyone, Armstrong 'liberated' the jazz improviser.

In Chicago some of the most famous names of early jazz began to perform and record. Armstrong formed his Hot Five and Hot Seven in Chicago in the 1920s, and Jelly Roll Morton his Red Hot Peppers, two of the finest bands in early jazz. The blues became popular in Chicago too, and a line of great blues singers was founded on the prominence of Bessie Smith's magnificent operatic voice. Young whites, too, continued to be active in developing hybrids of these ingredients.

The contrapuntal, collective style of improvisation gave way to an individualistic music in which the soloist is highlighted over accompaniment from a rhythm section. Of the soloists who rose during this period, the short-lived white trumpeter Bix Beiderbecke became perhaps the best known. Though he was part of a white jazz scene that

LEFT *The Empress of the Blues – Bessie Smith. She tragically died when the Depression had undermined the blues market, and before the 1940s saw its revival.*

BELOW LEFT *Mr Jelly Roll on piano – his ego was big, but so was his talent. Morton helped set the wheels of ensemble writing in motion.*

RIGHT *The Wolverines in 1925, a vehicle for the graceful and lyrical trumpet of Bix Beiderbecke (far right)*

BELOW *Sidney Bechet, a saxophone colossus. When John Coltrane heard his records, he said 'did all those old guys swing like that?'*

included both the pseudo-classicisms of Paul Whiteman and a variety of rhythmically stiff small groups, the ascetic gracefulness of his own contribution triumphed over all of it.

By the end of the Twenties, three saxophonists – Sidney Bechet, Johnny Hodges and Coleman Hawkins – were creating a music for the horn previously regarded as a sugary inferior of the clarinet. And Morton, Fletcher Henderson and Duke Ellington were beginning to demonstrate that jazz composition was not a contradiction in terms. Morton proved with his 1926 recordings that a New Orleans contrapuntal style could begin to suggest big-band techniques, beginning with the grouping of clarinet players into trios within the ensemble. Luis Russell took over the King Oliver Band in 1929 and the music signalled some of the ingredients of 'swing'. Fletcher Henderson's Dixie Stompers, between 1925 and 1928, began to join instruments together in groupings or 'sections', even though the line-up didn't run to more than ten musicians.

But it was Duke Ellington who redefined what was possible for a larger jazz ensemble, just as Louis Armstrong had redefined what was possible for an improviser. By the end of his half-century in jazz, Ellington had not only created an orchestral music that was more vigorous than most of what was produced in the same period by American classical composers, but he had developed a method of

principle of call and response. Benny Goodman's band seamlessly blended several of the developments of jazz up to that time – elements of New Orleans music, the Kansas riff style, and a clarity and deliberation of phrasing that came from conservatoire training, as in Goodman's case.

But the craze didn't last. At the end of the 1930s, a drummer called Kenny Clarke was getting himself fired from the Teddy Hill band for abandoning the trademark of swing drummers – the insistently booming on-the-beat bass drum – and transferring the timekeeping to the ride cymbal, which he claimed to be 'lighter and tastier'. But in 1940 Clarke found himself invited by Hill to form a band of young players at a run-down club on 108th Street called Minton's. Hill had been given the job of finding a suitable house band, and thought that the experimental players might have novelty value, and would probably come cheap. Clarke assembled pianist Thelonious Monk, bassist Nick Fenton and trumpeter Joe Guy. A Roy Eldridge-like trumpeter called Dizzy Gillespie began sitting in. And when Clarke and Monk went to hear an unknown young

LEFT *Armed with a huge tone and a musical education, Coleman Hawkins virtually created the role of the tenor saxophone in jazz.*

RIGHT *The fountainhead of advanced ideas on jazz composition – the elegant and mighty Duke Ellington.*

composition that sprang authentically from the very core of jazz itself. Many of Ellington's pieces were written with specific soloists in mind. Ellington's compositions, though rarely hits at the time, have become part of the musical tapestry of the century – songs like 'Creole Love Call', 'Mood Indigo' and 'Sophisticated Lady'. And orchestras from the 1930s on, that have depended on even a modicum of inspiration from jazz, have gone to Ellington's work as the fountainhead of ideas on the subject.

At the beginning of the Thirties, jazz music's second exodus began. Many of those who had left the southlands for Chicago moved on to New York. And as they did so a new idiom was founded – swing. It was a form of pop music that turned into an industry so massive that only the boom of rock 'n' roll in the 1950s topped it in the history of showbusiness.

Ellington was part of the swing age, although his music transcended it. But it was a characteristic of swing to feature big jazz orchestras. This significantly happened in New York and in Kansas City. The bands of Bennie Moten and Count Basie developed the 'riff' technique – a derivation of an African

saxophonist called Charlie Parker who was playing at an after-hours joint called Clark Monroe's Uptown House, they realized at once that he was not only on the same track as them but a long way further down it. Parker began to appear on the Minton's roster as well.

The new music developed in both the original swing sites – Kansas and Harlem. Charlie Parker had heard Count Basie's poetic tenorist, Lester Young, in the city's clubs, and for a while was obsessed with learning Young solos and cultivating that seagull-like floating delivery. He also taught himself all twelve keys and their related scales and chords, not knowing that jazz music traditionally only used a handful of them.

Like Armstrong, Parker stretched the beat, began and ended his solos in unexpected places, and was a terrifying player of blues. He also understood harmonic alternatives Armstrong could never have known, which gave him many more notes to choose from in any song. In much of his work, Parker seemed intent on playing all of them, but instead of making his music technical and impenetrable, in his hands it simply became more and more passionate

and expressive. The new idiom was dubbed 'rebop' and eventually 'bebop' – because of the sound of the 'scat-singing' required for a vocalist to try to replicate its melodies and phrasing.

But though the Minton's players are rightly regarded as founders of the movement, they all had their forerunners in swing players who had taken the harmonies and technical potential of their instruments close to the edge of the known world without actually pushing the lot over. Guitarist Charlie Christian did bridge both. He was a star soloist with the Benny Goodman band, and with recordings like 'Solo Flight' brought the newly invented electric guitar to the forefront of the music business.

The characteristics of bebop were a nervous speediness, a desire to say everything in the fastest and most concentrated way, with fragmented melodies, distortions and developments of the themes of old swing tunes reforged. Its practitioners were obsessed with the exclusion of the obvious. The pattern would

usually involve a unison chorus at the beginning and the end (generally played by the trumpet and the saxophone), a series of taut and concentrated choruses of soloing from all of the musicians in turn, and a return to the theme.

The emphasis in swing was on the first and third beats of a four-beat bar: *boom*-chick, *boom*-chick. Though jazz musicians had always interfered with this pattern and made unexpected departures from it, it was still the underlying source from which everything flowed. Chord changes tended to be made on the strong beats, phrases tended to begin and end there. It sounded, to most ears, 'natural'. With the arrival of bebop, the 'natural' laws were broken. Charlie Christian had been resolving phrases on the weak beats, as had Gillespie, and Charlie Parker was soon phrasing almost entirely around offbeats.

Inevitably, the challenging nature of bebop inspired a backlash and an affectionate look at the past.

Cab Calloway disliked bop and called it 'Chinese music'. Some critics saw it as the end of jazz and the start of some new form that had closer relations to modern 'serious' music. New Orleans styles were revived in the late Forties, and early pioneers like Bunk Johnson – whose music involved the pre-syncopation marching band rhythms – came back into favour.

There was another reaction to bop, one that didn't involve digging into the archives for jazz music's earliest origins. This was the development of the 'cool school'. Miles Davis, a young trumpeter who had worked with Charlie Parker, was a powerful influence on it, since he possessed a soft, introverted sound, was not given to furious scatter-gun effects like Gillespie, and was more at home on ballads or mid-tempo tunes than the breakneck tempos associated with early bop. Lester Young had semaphored this development at least a decade before in his soft, burnished, tightly distilled solos with Count Basie.

At New York's Royal Roost in 1948, Miles Davis put together an orchestra of his own. It didn't hold together for long, but was recorded the following year. The sound it made was almost as startling a transformation of what had gone before it as bebop was of swing. The orchestrations were plush, yielding, lustrous. The solos seemed to emerge from the background as if drifting in and out of a morning mist. The sound of that band established a tone and pattern for much of the work done by the younger jazz musicians in the first part of the post-war period.

Gil Evans, a white arranger intrigued by Duke Ellington, who had emerged from the Claude Thornhill band, a superior dance band, had much to

BELOW *Miles Davis, 1960s vintage – a trumpet soloist of taste and restrained passion, and a musical thinker of restless vision.*

ABOVE *Arranger Gil Evans' lustrous 1940s' orchestral work was described as 'clouds of sound'. In the 1970s and 1980s he was adapting Jimi Hendrix, among others. A master of tone colour, whatever the idiom.*

do with the creation of these 'clouds of sound', an effect he is still capable of eliciting today. Only the orchestra of the altoist and clarinettist Woody Herman, frequently touching on Europeanisms through a talented arranger called Ralph Burns, had much inclination towards a similar territory.

There was another white input that was also running in this direction, but on a parallel rather than a convergent line. Lennie Tristano, a blind piano player from Chicago with a highly developed theoretical background, literally founded a school of his own – the 'New School of Music'. Adherents to Tristano's precepts included altoist Lee Konitz (who was also involved with the Davis orchestra recordings), tenorist Warne Marsh and guitarist Billy Bauer.

This movement went a long way towards concurrently developing the image of the white hipster –

undemonstratively enjoying a subdued, analytical and intellectual music, fascinated by structure and disinterested in explicit emotional highs and lows. But Tristano's objectives were not to purge jazz of emotion. He simply wished to liberate the music from slavish commitment to the harmonies of souped-up standards, in which respect he uncannily foresaw the 'free jazz' developments of a decade later.

This trend towards classical purity was resisted by the generation of beboppers that followed the pioneers. Groups led by drummers Max Roach and Art Blakey, by pianist Horace Silver, and featuring dynamic soloists like Lee Morgan, Sonny Rollins, Clifford Brown and the young John Coltrane, performed a bop descendant usually called 'hard bop'. The complicated harmonies of the cool school were comfortably absorbed by the hard bop players, but what Marshall Stearns called 'the posture of

LEFT *A high priest of hard bop, drummer Art Blakey has been leading versions of his Jazz Messengers since the 1950s – musicians like Wayne Shorter and Wynton Marsalis made their reputations with Blakey.*

BELOW LEFT *The Chopin of jazz piano – the romantic and reflective Bill Evans, whose delicacy nevertheless disguised robustness and swing.*

RIGHT *One of the all-time great tenorists and a great jazz eccentric too. Sonny Rollins was a cornerstone of hard bop, but his music is full of humour and bizarre references.*

BELOW RIGHT *Dave Brubeck's band was a rare jazz box office success in the 1950s and early 1960s, with hit tunes like 'Take Five'.*

resignation' vanished. This music was vibrant, assertive, vigorous. And a music somewhere between the two, with elements of bebop but also of 'cool' music and a more ambiguous structure based on scales rather than chords – like Indian music – was adopted by Miles Davis, John Coltrane and pianist Bill Evans for a milestone recording of 1960 called 'Kind of Blue'.

As if in response to such 'chamber jazz', there then came a new twist that could be absorbed by the commercial music world. Horace Silver in particular, but also most of the principal hard boppers, recovered an old respect for the blues, that tributary that had fed jazz so generously and productively a half-century before. Silver developed a way of

playing on the beat that coined the expression 'funk'.

'Soul' music, a style taken from gospel and the sounds of the black churches, found a powerful conduit in the voice and piano style of Ray Charles. In mood and atmosphere, funk and soul were the opposite end of the universe to 'cool' music. Where the latter symbolized isolation, deliberation, reflectiveness and the exercise of the intellect, the former implied gregariousness, optimism, even hedonism. Soul music and then funk in succession operated a powerful pull on the popular music of the Sixties and Seventies.

A manageable derivation of bop had become highly marketable at the end of the Fifties. The Dave Brubeck group and John Lewis's Modern Jazz

Quartet played sell-out concerts all over the world. Brubeck delivered an ornate, semi-classical jazz that blended improvisation with complex time signatures; the M.J.Q. (a piano-and-vibes-led quartet) played a sophisticated and elegant version that had some ingredients of the 'cool school', but a way with quiet blues and standards that stood four-square in an earthier jazz tradition.

But at the beginning of the Sixties, jazz experienced what the world of concert and conservatoire music had experienced with the arrival of composers like Schoenberg and Webern and the serialists – a departure from conventional tonality, from the lattice-work of music provided by the orthodox scale and its vernacular, 'bent-note' derivations through jazz. As in the concert world, the shock-wave in the world of jazz was substantial – maybe more so than there had been when bop first reared its head. Free

jazz hit jazz fans reared on this music as if a door had suddenly been flung open in their faces and a hurricane roared in.

For the free players, hard bop had already ossified. They were bored with its routine opening and closing choruses, its orderly procession of soloists, what they saw as its treadmill of harmonic patterns. The avantists salvaged from the early days of jazz a principle that had been abandoned with the Chicago school – collective improvisation, several horns intertwined to produce a 'group solo' not actually conceived in its entirety by any individual.

But the similarity between the impact of free music in the Sixties and atonality in the Twenties began and ended in the decision to break out of formal bonds. The route taken by Shoenberg was into a careful reconstruction of the elements of the scale. Jazz musicians did it in a far more spontaneous, untutored, and in some respects romantic and haphazard manner. Sometimes pieces would hover around 'tonal centres', but as often as not be completely free of any recognized landmark. The latter approach sometimes produced music of scorching intensity, but also engendered as much

repetition as existed in the styles it was subverting.

Jazz in this period was thus loosening its connections with the European harmonic principles on which it was founded. It was therefore becoming less a music of the New World, more a World Music – since the musics of cultures other than the European had long depended on different subdivisions of the scale, different concepts of time and organization, different instrumentation. These ingredients began to be objects of study for the leading avant-garde jazz players.

John Coltrane was from North Carolina, Ornette Coleman is a Texan. Though their beginnings in music occurred at much the same time, it was years before Coleman's work was acknowledged as serious, or even competent. Coltrane, a powerful technician on tenor from his youth (he had received some conservatory musical training) and comfortable with the conventional styles at the start of his career, was able to command regular work from his 21st year.

Both began in rhythm 'n' blues bands. Coltrane had a succession of these gigs, including work with Eddie 'Cleanhead' Vinson, Earl Bostic and Johnny

ABOVE LEFT *John Lewis' Modern Jazz Quartet was as precise and meticulous as a Swiss watch, and set high standards for 'chamber jazz'.*

ABOVE *John Coltrane's famous 'A Love Supreme' sold a quarter of a million copies. A soulful and technically breathtaking player, Coltrane saw himself on a musical mission.*

ABOVE RIGHT *Long tall Dexter – Dexter Gordon's dramatic tenor sound influenced Coltrane, and Gordon even starred in an excellent jazz movie, Bertrand Tavernier's Round Midnight.*

Hodges before joining Miles Davis in 1955, a crucial step in his career. Coleman, who had taught himself the instrument – and mostly 'wrongly' in the formal sense – had no such acceptance from fellow musicians and was frequently ridiculed for his odd tone and even odder harmonic sense. But by the time Coleman had made an impact and cut his first records, John Coltrane was already regarded as part of the front rank of the new saxophone players in jazz.

Coltrane had started as an altoist, under Charlie Parker's influence. The stints with the blues bands led him to switch to tenor, and Dexter Gordon became a model. When he joined Miles Davis in 1955, he was a more than competent hard bop saxophonist, and in 1957 he joined pianist Thelonious Monk at New York's Five Spot club. During this long engagement Coltrane maintained that he learned an immeasurable amount about harmonics from one of its most wayward and maverick practitioners.

By the same period Ornette Coleman had begun to be noticed, but the route to recognition had been very different. Coleman's self-teaching had engendered some idiosyncrasies, but principally the conviction that chord-based improvising (which Hawkins and Parker had been giants of and which Coltrane was devotedly pursuing still further) was limiting for improvisers.

Coleman began to work out his ensemble ideas in partnership with trumpeter Don Cherry (see page 100). Modern Jazz Quartet bassist Percy Heath played with Coleman, and got the saxophonist and the trumpeter to attend the jazz summer school run at Lenox, Massachusetts. A number of significant figures in the jazz world heard Coleman there, and

LEFT *Ornette Coleman's early contemporaries thought he couldn't play because he ignored conventional harmony. His work, which encouraged improvisors to play more intuitively, has since been adapted for chamber groups and symphony orchestras as well as jazz musicians.*

BELOW *Though in his 40s, Miles Davis came close to pop stardom with his jazz-rock 'fusion' bands in the late 1960s. Elaborate percussion and rhythm effects almost eclipsed the pre-eminence of the soloist.*

were immediately enthusiastic. This led to a gig at the Five Spot in New York in November 1959. The reaction was immediate. Some embraced this new music as the salvation for jazz, the way out of the harmonic impasse. Many dismissed it out of hand as chaotic and meaningless noise.

It soon became clear that Coleman's impact on jazz wasn't going to begin and end with a change in a saxophonist's approach to soloing, substantial though that was. Coleman had ideas about the future of jazz right across the board. In 1960 he made an album for Atlantic Records called 'Free Jazz', the modernism of which was endorsed by the reproduction of Jackson Pollock's 'White Light' on the cover. Dependence on pre-arrangement was minimal; there were no chords or bar-lines, and the instrumentalists soloed in turn, the others improvising 'accompaniments', but with the aim of avoiding orthodox harmony.

It was greeted by the public with mixed feelings, but as a standard-bearer for free collective improvisation, it inspired a generation of free-players that followed. Ironically – because at the time greeted

with five-star accolades in America's *Downbeat* but unrecognized on his home turf – there was in Britain a West Indian saxophonist called Joe Harriott who had been independently exploring very similar territory to Coleman, using written themes but developing improvisation between the members of the band collectively. Harriott prematurely died before his contribution was ever much remarked on.

In the mid-Sixties John Coltrane recorded the most influential record in his career, and one that influenced the course of many others. 'A Love Supreme', a simple, incantatory religious theme based on a four-note chant and improvised on modally, sold a quarter of a million copies. 'A Love Supreme' was released in 1965. Its appeal was not simply to jazz fans, but the fans of the psychedelic rock cult of the 1960s, in which lengthy modal improvisation over a minimal backing was normal and pop-song orientation was down-played.

The free-jazz upsurge was nothing short of a revolution. It didn't always have precise aims, it broke a lot of eggs in the course of making its omelette, but it demonstrated the potential for resisting the imposing weight of the European traditions. If what followed it would be a reforged free music that reintroduced many of the traditional elements but in rebuilt forms, then it would have done its job no less well. And this is more or less what happened.

The 1970s thus produced a wider range of parallel jazz-influenced musics than ever before. The rock 'n' roll born in the Fifties had developed a more exploratory turn in the hands of some musicians – notably in bands of the era like Cream and Soft Machine – and the techniques of jazz players were absorbed into an idiom that became known as 'jazz-rock' or 'fusion'. The mainstream of rejuvenated or preserved earlier styles – by now including hard bop – continued. Free jazz refined its vocabulary and musicians organized to protect and develop it – for example the Association for the Advancement of Creative Musicians in Chicago. This group was led by a brilliant orthodox pianist who had immersed himself in free playing – Muhal Richard Abrams. The other members of the organization were virtually all highly skilled conventional players who had taken to free music as a way out of what they saw as the trap of orthodox harmony and time.

The version of jazz that made the biggest impact in the late Sixties and early Seventies was certainly jazz-rock fusion. It made use of new elements – particularly electronics, electric bass-guitars and amplified drums – and it attempted to create a new kind of jazz that blended extensive improvisation with ornate and highly decorative versions of rock and funk rhythm playing. Even the traditional jazz instrumentation started to sound different. Miles Davis's trumpet around 1970 was processed by electronics in such a way as to take on much of the sound quality of an electric guitar. In 1969 and 1970, Davis released two key records – 'In a Silent Way' and 'Bitches Brew'; a fusion band called Weather Report was formed from a nucleus of some ex-Davis sidemen; and British guitarist John McLaughlin (who had also played with Davis) formed a more conventionally melodic and less electronic band called the Mahavishnu Orchestra.

Jazz-rock didn't last in popularity, never getting as big as the biggest booms in rock music had been. It appealed principally to middle-class, college-educated, and primarily white audiences, and the limitations it imposed on improvisation quickly dimmed the appeal of the idiom for jazz fans. Free music, which had gone on being practised around the world by all kinds of players throughout the 1970s, continued to flourish in a small way, and fed ideas back into the mainstream. And a variety of musical influences from many cultures around the world increasingly fed into jazz – from Latin America, from Africa, from the Middle East and from India. The ex-Ornette Coleman sideman, Don Cherry, embodies this breadth of view. The musical cultures of Tibet, China, India and Bali all surface in his work.

And at the end of the 1970s bebop – which had never really gone away – started to make its reappearance with a vengeance. In Britain at the beginning of the 1980s, black youth with time on their hands in a returned era of high unemployment developed styles of dancing that fitted even the fastest tempos of bebop.

A film, 'Absolute Beginners', was made in Britain, featuring some of these dancers and with a score composed by Gil Evans. A young London tenor saxophonist, Courtney Pine, had a bestselling album with a mixture of the hard, incantatory style of the classic John Coltrane quartet and elements of hard bop. And fittingly, the return of the music brought new work opportunities for original bop musicians who had been around for years – like Art Blakey and Johnny Griffin. It was hard to tell whether they were more delighted than their young audiences that this enthusiastic encounter had actually come about.

LEFT *British guitarist John McLaughlin was another popular exponent of fusion. A brilliant technician, McLaughlin later returned to more orthodox jazz and to acoustic instruments.*

LEFT *If 'world music' is anything more than a flag of convenience, Don Cherry is one of its pioneers. A one-time partner of Ornette Coleman, Cherry's influences now come from the East as much as from Afro-America.*

BELOW *British jazz star of the 1980s, Courtney Pine. He proved that hit records and tough improvisation did not have to be mutually exclusive.*

CHAPTER TWO

JAZZ VOICES

> ‘ The songs can tell your life story
> for you, can’t they? ’

ADELAIDE HALL TO KITTY GRIME

Of all the ways in which jazz breaks the rules of accepted European standards of excellence, the most fundamental of the musical instruments – the human voice – broke them first, and has resolutely gone on breaking them through all of the music’s kaleidoscopic changes of style. Even in her decline, when her voice was a shadow of what it had been, Billie Holiday remained one of the most expressive of jazz singers. Because, as a jazz singer, she was

Mahalia Jackson, the most dignified, powerful and moving of gospel singers. Reluctant to be identified with jazz, she nevertheless worked memorably with Louis Armstrong and Duke Ellington.

supposed to express herself, and not be a conduit for the sensibilities of a stranger, her music still told a story in her declining years, in some ways the most poignant and moving story of all.

In West Africa singing has traditionally been a part of everyday life, not simply a diversion from it, an entertainment, or a purely aesthetic pursuit. It has been an aspect of speech, a means of emphasizing or intensifying a statement, a means of confirming a communal spirit, a means of making work pass more quickly and painlessly. Work songs were thus encouraged by slave owners, in Africa and in the Americas and the Caribbean. Richard F. Burton wrote from Central Africa in 1860 that ‘the fisherman will accompany his paddle, the porter his trudge, the housewife her task of rubbing down grain, with song'. The tempo and the spirit of the song were governed by the work in hand.

White singers and entertainers in the 19th century quickly adapted a version of the work songs, gospel music and spirituals of the railroads and plantations, blacked-up to give themselves both an element of authenticity and an opportunity for a cheap laugh, and established a genre of 'nigger-minstrel' music that dated from the end of the 18th century. A song written by Thomas Dartmouth 'Daddy' Rice, a blackface entertainer, in 1818, entered the language: the title of the song included the words 'Jim Crow'.

After the Civil War and emancipation, life changed for the ex-slaves but didn't necessarily improve. For the remainder of the 19th century the work song and the field holler slowly changed into the blues – an angry, personal, frequently resigned musical observation on the many faces of oppression. The other strand of black music was the more robust, jaunty and accessible kind that had emerged from

LEFT *Mamie Smith, the first singer to record a blues. 'Crazy Blues' surprised Okeh Records by selling 100,000 copies in the early 1920s.*

ABOVE *Realism, resourcefulness and sheer power – the magnificent blues voice of Bessie Smith.*

minstrelsy in the hands of travelling players. This was based on the harmonic and melodic ideas of Europe more than Africa, but its rhythmic foundation was syncopation.

White singers' performances in blackface 'nigger-minstrel' acts popularized the style first of all, though Jelly Roll Morton, a passable singer, had made some impact with it. But it was the famous white artists, particularly the Russian Jewish émigrés, Sophie Tucker and Al Jolson, who took a version of the style on to Broadway, into American homes and eventually all over the world. Jolson's father had been a synagogue cantor, and his own music mingled the ragtime tradition and light opera. His phrasing and style influenced a number of significant singers who followed – notably the brilliant Ethel Waters, Bing Crosby and Connee Boswell.

Parallel with minstrelsy, but a later development of work songs and of much more substantial significance to jazz, was the blues. Ma Rainey was the first blues singer of real substance to get national recogni-

tion in America, though she didn't record until three years after the first singer to make a blues disc, Mamie Smith. Rainey believed that she first heard the blues in 1902, and featured blues as the finale to her vaudeville act. The songs were earthy, sombre, powerful and dignified – as can be heard on tracks like 'Jelly Bean Blues', 'Counting the Blues' and 'See See Rider', and the recordings feature her in tandem with vigorous accompanists like Louis Armstrong and Tommy Ladnier.

Following Rainey came Bessie Smith, the best known blues singer of all. She came from Chattanooga, Tennessee, and was in showbusiness by the age of nine, discovered in a tent show by Ma Rainey and taken on as a member of her troupe. Possessed of a powerful contralto, successfully merging the folk and vaudeville strands, and exhibiting both fierce swing and an unfettered emotional freedom, Bessie Smith always sounded sorrowful yet unsentimental. Her voice possessed a granite-like toughness, articulating an unflinching realism, ironic pragmatism and absence of sentiment. Her most famous recordings with the young Louis Armstrong included 'J.C. Holmes Blues', 'Careless Love' and 'Reckless Blues' and with the more respectful Tommy Ladnier on the chilling 'Dyin' By the Hour'.

Fashions shifted on Bessie Smith's career, for all her genius; by the end of the 1920s, a less earthy and pragmatic version of the idiom was in demand. In 1931 Columbia Records dropped Smith from its roster. She remained in relative obscurity, touring the South once again, until the wealthy jazz enthusiast John Hammond rediscovered her and brought her back to the studios in 1933. This date with Benny Goodman, Jack Teagarden and others produced more classics including 'Gimme A Pigfoot' and 'Do Your Duty'.

Her first hits in 1923 had topped 750,000 record sales and saved the Columbia company from bankruptcy. But the records were almost all bought by blacks, and after the Depression fashions changed; she was lucky to scrape sales of 3,000 for her final recordings.

Through the 1930s Smith attempted to adjust her style to the demands of the swing era. But she never got a chance to claim the fruits of the revival of early jazz and blues that occurred in the 1940s. She died on the way to hospital following a car crash while on tour in the South in 1937 – reports that she had been unable to gain admission to a white hospital turned out to be hearsay. It was, however, understandable hearsay given the circumstances in the Deep South at the time.

Of the men, the first blues singers to gain a reputation were Blind Lemon Jefferson and Huddie Leadbetter or 'Leadbelly', both of them continuing a tradition of singing that came direct from the railroads and plantations. Following them came Robert Johnson, Big Bill Broonzy, Son House, Muddy Waters and many other more urbanized practitioners including those who enjoyed some belated success in the rhythm 'n' blues boom of the Sixties – like Memphis Slim, Sonny Boy Williamson, Howlin Wolf and John Lee Hooker. And that boom also brought with it a new generation of authentic American blues singers – like Buddy Guy, B.B. King and Otis Rush.

Some of the blues singers joined the swing and big band movement. Jimmy Rushing from Oklahoma joined the Basie band in the 1930s, and there was a general tendency for the Texas traditions of blues and those of the Kansas and Midwest-based swing bands to mingle. The other strand of blues migration was from Mississippi to Chicago, which is why that town became such a vibrant home of a mutated rural into blues singing. Joe Williams, another powerful blues artist, took Rushing's place in the Basie band in the 1950s.

And it was Big Joe Turner who perhaps had the most substantial influence of all of them. Because he had worked with boogie-woogie pianists in the Thirties – musicians who had evolved a highly rhythmic form of piano playing based on blues chords – Turner had helped develop a variation of the idiom that combined the raw and vibrant vocal style with an animated, driving beat. The similarities between this and the rock 'n' roll that emerged in the Fifties is too obvious to need explaining. Turner

wrote one of the early rock hits 'Shake, Rattle and Roll'. It was white artists, however, who reaped the rewards from it.

Broader than the blues, but locked into the heart of jazz, was Louis Armstrong, as imaginative a singer as he was a trumpeter. Armstrong's warmth, affability and melodic audacity, and the intense swing that he injected into everything he did, virtually founded the song-line of jazz vocalists. He also invented 'scat' in the early 1920s, a type of wordless singing in the form of accents and instrument-like phrasing.

With Billie Holiday the transformation of the jazz singer from the earthy majesty and booming projection of a singer like Bessie Smith was complete. Where Smith was declamatory, fierce and challenging, Holiday was quiet and delicate, her effects dependent on sophisticated twists and turns of

ABOVE *The peerless Lady Day. Billie Holiday's bruised, intimate style was the quintessence of jazz, reshaping the song in the image of the singer.*

LEFT *A giant of urban blues, ex-Kansas City barman Big Joe Turner. White rock hits like 'Shake, Rattle and Roll' were his work.*

RIGHT *Singing was not just a second string to Louis Armstrong, but a means of expression as rich and varied as his trumpet sound.*

LEFT *Ella Fitzgerald – swing, range, energy and wit.*

ABOVE *Betty Carter, the closest singer to a bebop saxophone currently at work, and a performer of highly*

original phrasing and intonation.

RIGHT *The formidable Sarah Vaughan, possessor of the most complete vocal technique of all surviving jazz singers.*

phrasing. But though she became a peerless popular singer, it was founded on the intimacy of her feeling for jazz. Popularity didn't separate her from an inevitably bitter acquaintance with the racial issue either, and with the song 'Strange Fruit' (a reference to lynched blacks, hanging from the trees of the southlands), Billie Holiday recorded one of the most resounding condemnations of racism in the history of American popular music.

The other factor that changed the course of jazz singing and which Billie Holiday was particularly well-disposed to take advantage of was a piece of technology now taken for granted in popular music and jazz – the microphone. Much of the uniqueness of Billie Holiday could not be detected without the mike, except in very intimate surroundings or in the course of the technique she frequently used of singing to members of her audience in turn in venues that made this possible, by singing directly to each of the tables.

Holiday's life was just about as racked by the contradictions of the racial situation as anyone's in the history of jazz. Singing with the all-black Count Basie Orchestra, she had to black up in the South because her skin was light and the authorities would come down hard on what they saw as a 'mixed' band. With Artie Shaw's white outfit, the opposite was true and she was condemned to a life separated from her fellow musicians, eating apart, rooming apart, using separate entrances to the venues. Billie Holiday died at 44 in 1959.

Ella Fitzgerald was a product of the same period,

but her career followed a different path. Discovered as a teenager at the Apollo Theater in Harlem, she won a stint with the Chick Webb band as a prize in a talent contest. Staying with them, she briefly became their leader after Webb's death in 1939. Fitzgerald continues to be a singer of infectious energy, elegance and swing, though the extent to which she remakes songs in her own image is not comparable with Holiday – not a weakness, but grounds for contending that she, like Frank Sinatra, is an inspired pop singer rather than a true jazz improviser.

With the birth of bebop came another strain. Bop was difficult ground for singers. Its tortuous melodic twists and turns defeated all but the most agile. Billy Eckstine, a great fan of the new idiom who also earned himself the title of the first black pop idol, ran a band in which many of the leading figures of bop got the chance to play the way they wanted to. In the Fifties and Sixties, Lambert, Hendricks and Ross developed a style of scatting bebop out of early experiments in vocalizing Count Basie records, and eventually put lyrics to tunes derived from the solos of Charlie Parker, Lester Young, Sonny Rollins and others.

Sarah Vaughan, Carmen McRae and Betty Carter were all female singers influenced by bebop. Vaughan is a singer with an operatic range and a facility for mixing high-class popular entertainment with penetrating – and sometimes unnerving – reworkings of songs that can make a standard like 'Summertime' glow with fresh life. Carter followed Dinah Washington into the Lionel Hampton band in the 1940s, and it was as a blues singer that she initially found her place, though she later became one of the most highly skilled 'instrumental' singers in jazz, and continues to be. June Christy, Mary Ann McCall and Anita O'Day came out of the big bands.

Among the men, Mark Murphy has developed a warm and humorous contemporary style out of the mainstream swing band vocalist's tradition. Gil Scott Heron has brought poetry and politics to the art. And finally, the most recently successful of all of them – Al Jarreau. Jarreau quotes his influences as Billie Holiday, Nat Cole and Lambert, Hendricks and Ross. Like an even younger arrival, Bobby McFerrin, Jarreau is capable of sounding like an entire band, and can mimic the sounds of saxes, drums, trumpets and bass lines at will.

Also worth remembering are Dakota Staton, Helen Merrill, Nina Simone, Nancy Wilson and Sheila Jordan. Simone particularly has found a special place in contemporary music, despite the ups and downs of her professional life and the tension between her music and her constant battles with Tin Pan Alley and its values. Her voice is brittle, uncompromising, frequently moving and sometimes the vehicle for a bitter exposition of the circumstances of black Americans. And gospel music, under the towering influence of Mahalia Jackson, helped bring soul into being as a branch of pop. This brought singers like Tina Turner, Diana

Ross and Aretha Franklin to the fore.

In the field of free music there are Britons like Norma Winstone, Julie Tippetts and Maggie Nicols, the Pole Urzula Dudziak and the Greek Diamanda Galas. With these singers an entirely new range of sounds enters the musical language. They are as likely to moan, scream, gibber or harangue as they are to deliver a rounded melodic line or an identifiable lyric. But their expressiveness is not diminished, merely of another kind.

ABOVE *Devastating technician Bobby McFerrin, who can sound like an entire jazz or funk band with no more props than a standard mike.*

LEFT *Passionate, brittle and uncompromising, the art of Nina Simone is a highwire act that has audiences on the edge of their seats.*

RIGHT *Aretha Franklin, the carrier of Mahalia Jackson's torch and a massively popular blues and soul star.*

CHAPTER THREE

ROCKIN' IN RHYTHM

' The drum is the mother of the music, it's
like the heartbeat. It transmits the pulse, the
energy, the basic feeling *'*

DRUMMER ANDREW CYRILLE

African drumming is one of the most sophisticated forms of percussion music in the world. Since African languages are far more dependent on pitch, timbre and timing than European ones, it's possible for drumming to take on many of the expressive characteristics of the spoken language. As experts have insisted, African 'talking' drumming is thus not a form of Morse code: it is a mutated form of speech.

Of all the early beboppers, Art Blakey remains the most instantly recognizable. His playing is heated and exuberant, and his press rolls whoosh into life like fireworks.

The history of jazz drums is the story of its emancipation from the marching military band, which was where it had its origins in New Orleans.

French critic André Hodeir's description of the way that the black musicians borrowed the principle of the two- and four-beat bar structures from European music – used in hymns, polkas and marches – is a good summary of the restless urge to experiment that has characterized jazz. 'Just like someone trying to find the most comfortable position in a new bed', Hodeir wrote, the black American musician 'experimented with different ways of accommodating himself to the space between measure bars'.

The first conception of rhythm for the jazz musician was thus the military march and the polka. Early on, the polka's offbeats began to be mingled with march time. The variations on this that were established by the early jazz drummers Warren 'Baby' Dodds, Zutty Singleton and Kaiser Marshall, still depended heavily on establishing the main beat as a boom-boom on the bass drum, with the snare drum for accents and shading on the offbeats.

Around 1933, the structure on which jazz music was based began to change. The old march and polka rhythms had been based on a two-beat formula; now a four-beat structure emerged to replace this, displacing with it what Hodeir had called 'the waddling character of the New Orleans rhythm'. The Count Basie orchestra perfected the playing of a rhythm of four equal beats, and the sound became synonymous with swing.

Gene Krupa was the first drum virtuoso. His solos were events, and eventually the bands he played in became primarily showcases for his drum displays, a tradition that was followed by Mel Lewis, Buddy Rich and Louie Bellson. Also to emerge from the swing and big band era was another white drummer, Dave Tough, who came from the Tommy Dorsey band and whose subtlety and swing helped to found the complex principles of modern jazz. So did Count Basie's drummer, Jo Jones.

LEFT *Count Basie's most famous drummer, the mercurial Jo Jones. Jones did much to found the Basie legend of effortless, floating swing.*

RIGHT *Gene Krupa, the first to make a virtuoso display of the drum solo. Krupa founded a showbiz tradition that continued through Buddy Rich, Mel Lewis and Louie Bellson.*

BELOW RIGHT *Warren 'Baby' Dodds, one of the leading New Orleans drummers, and an accompanist for the city's major talents including Louis Armstrong, King Oliver and Jimmy Noone.*

BELOW *Dave Tough, a subtle, intelligent and much-admired drummer whose playing bridged swing and bebop.*

That Jones 'played like the wind' became a commonplace in jazz conversation. He had an effortless, driving beat, his use of the hi-hat to maintain the pulse was as good as or better than anyone in jazz, and his adaptability behind soloists bordered on the psychic. In addition, Jones, like Sid Catlett and Dave Tough, could be as exhilarating on brushes as with sticks, a technique more usually suited to downplaying the drummer's role to a hushed and reverential assistance.

Jones was descended from the direct line that led from Baby Dodds to Chick Webb, Big Sid Catlett, Cozy Cole and Lionel Hampton. Catlett, a preserver of the Zutty Singleton tradition of excellent time-keeping, discreet use of press rolls for emphasis, but not much more self-aggrandizement than that, was the ideal accompanist. He would use a light cymbal beat behind a clarinet, a loose, splashy hi-hat behind a trombone and a closed, clapping one behind a piano. His bass drumming, which frequently used offbeats, was ahead of its time.

But the swing tradition of drumming continued way beyond the 'swing era'. Its most emphatic and technically astonishing defender was Buddy Rich, who continued to play (despite ill health) into his late sixties and hung his act on some of the most complex and barnstorming drum performances in all the history of jazz. Rich, who was capable of executing as effective a drum roll with one hand as many practitioners were with two, had the activities of his left hand described by Whitney Balliett as being 'as furious as an electric typewriter'.

With the contrast between Cole and Jones, it's possible to hear the evolution of drums from the staccato, beat-oriented accompanist style of the early period to the even and responsive style of swing and the borderline of modern jazz. The hi-hat (a contraption devised by placing two small cymbals face to face on an upright and rhythmically clapping them together by means of a pedal) was used by both Jones and Tough as a means of carrying the principle beat and liberating the rest of the drumkit for shading, accents and response to the musical events elsewhere in the band.

The beats in the four-bar unit were by now being evened out. We have seen in the previous chapter how 'swing' developed as a more sophisticated and urbane kind of jazz, dependent on big orchestral

effects and the massive enhancement of the role of the soloist – a line derived from Chicago styles. A smoothness and streamlined vigour had entered the music that had taken nothing away from its vitality and power to surprise. Jones became a defender of the even four-beats-in-a-bar percussion style. And with Kenny Clarke – the man who, more than any, created the bridge from swing to bebop – the freeing of the kit for a more 'improvisatory' role on the part of the drummer became even more advanced. Where the natural subdivision of rhythm was the quarter-note for Cozy Cole, it was the eighth for Clarke.

Clarke himself said, 'I played rhythm patterns, and they were superimposed over the regular beat.' These patterns would also be scattered rather than played regularly as in swing, the snare and bass drums providing accents between the beats rather than enhancing any of those imparting the basic 'pulse'. Subjectively, this meant an *implication* of the beat rather than explicit expression of it in many cases, leading to more ambiguity and nuance in the music.

Max Roach, the most advanced of all the bebop drummers, once said that his ambition was 'to do with rhythm what Bach did with melody'. It was a good summary of the multi-layered approach of these drummers, superimposing a variety of rhythms upon each other, making the rhythms vary with the musical developments and making the drums more expressive. Closer, in fact, to the African drumming which had otherwise been mostly coarsened and simplified by its migration into jazz. Roach played out-of-meter patterns against the basic beat more adventurously than any of the others in the first generation of bebop – so much so that it was initially difficult to believe that only one drummer was at work. Roach has carried this even to the extent of forming all-drum bands, as did Art Blakey in the 1950s.

Blakey is one of the most irrepressible, vigorous and earthy of all jazz drummers. The wild, effusive quality of his playing stems frequently from unfettered cymbal splashes, volcanic eruptions of press rolls behind soloists and at the end of choruses and a boiling beat. Roach influenced Blakey's play-ing, but so did Sid Catlett – and the effect of the Catlett influence on the Roach one was to make Blakey sound more dramatic and subtle in the use of dynamics.

Philly Joe Jones merged the impulsiveness of Blakey with the knowledge and deliberation of Roach. His playing exhibited some of the business-like sustaining of swing that the earlier drummers had done, though intensifying excitement through excursions into double-time patterns. And his intro-ductions, as he revealed in a stint with pianist Bill Evans, could be masterpieces of surprise.

LEFT *Buddy Rich, a box-office hit wherever he went. Even those who disliked his big-band's showy music admired Rich's extraordinary technique.*

TOP *Kenny 'Klook' Clarke, one of the founders of bebop. He sought to make the placing of the beat more ambiguous, to reduce the predictability of swing.*

ABOVE *Max Roach, the most complex of the bebop first wave. Roach's early work suggested several drummers playing at once, his playing being virtually a counterpoint of contrasting meters.*

Hard bop brought its own crop of drummers – notably Roy Haynes, Dannie Richmond, Louis Hayes and Elvin Jones. Jones particularly was the next revolutionary. He took the practice of shifting the basic beat to the cymbals or hi–hat and refined it further, so that it became increasingly difficult to tell where the 'marking' of the beat actually lay.

In the forefront of the new jazz of the Sixties there were thus three principal stances among drummers. Coltrane's band moved to the spacious, majestic 'unplaced' beat of Elvin Jones. Miles Davis's hung on Tony Williams's dense, crowded and clattery playing, which was a less ambiguous development of Elvin Jones. Ornette Coleman, however, who had revolutionized the approach to harmony as a basis for improvisation, used at various times three drummers who were all experts in a more conventional mapping out of basic beats. Billy Higgins, Ed Blackwell and Charles Moffett – particularly the first two – were possessed of a light touch, an open and uncluttered style and a sparing but unfailingly swinging use of accents that established clear links to far earlier figures of jazz drumming.

There was a fourth tributary of the 1960s avant-garde. When Albert Ayler was reintroducing many of the folk-memories of jazz into the avant-garde, his drummer, Sunny Murray, was behaving as if those simple, folksy tunes weren't actually present at all. Murray developed a way of swinging without conventional beat or measure, and his cymbal beat, far from being a stream of distinct, if high-speed percussive blows, sounded like steam escaping from a boiler.

Many other drummers followed in this style – like Phillip Wilson (a brilliant performer who had played in the Paul Butterfield Blues Band), Steve McCall, Don Moye and Ronald Shannon Jackson. In Europe's free scene, Han Bennink and Pierre Favre were dominant, followed in their turn by Englishmen Tony Oxley (who uses electronic percussion as well as a conventional jazz kit) and John Stevens, German Paul Lovens, and Finn Edward Vesala. Many of the European players use both Murray-esque 'free' patterns and pastiches of older styles in their work.

With the rise of 'jazz rock' and 'fusion' music, a return to an older and simpler beat occurred, though

the means of playing it was often highly ornate and complex. Where from bebop onwards the cymbals had become all important and the remainder of the kit principally of use for accents, jazz-rock time brought the second back to the tom-toms and bass drum. Alphonse Mouzon and Billy Cobham in particular became early stars of this approach.

As jazz has consolidated the effects of the changes of the Sixties and Seventies, drummers have appeared who can play in almost any idiom. One of the most impressive is Jack De Johnette, who worked with Bill Evans and in the early Miles Davis electric bands. De Johnette's bass drumming borders on a press roll, his cymbal sound has a stinging, whiplash quality and in general his playing imparts energy but with relaxation.

Ronald Shannon Jackson on the other hand, who came to the fore with the later incarnations of Ornette Coleman's electric bands, deploys rhythms from jazz, funk, reggae, even classical music – not separately, but in one drenching, constantly shifting wall of percussive noise. The effect, unexpectedly, can be witty, spirited and genuinely uplifting to flagging soloists.

LEFT *Elvin Jones further modified the displacement of the beat that had been performed by Kenny Clarke and the beboppers. Though Jones' pulse is always strong, it is not explicitly marked out but constantly shifts.*

ABOVE *Edward Blackwell has been most closely associated with Ornette Coleman and latterly Don Cherry. Light and crystal clear, his favourite touch is a sudden delicate rat-tat-tat of accents on the snare drum.*

ABOVE RIGHT *British drummer Tony Oxley came to fame as a bebop drummer with a highly unusual notion of cymbal patterns, later branching into contemporary composition and free-improvising.*

RIGHT *Ronald Shannon Jackson, a partner of Ornette Coleman and a major figure of 'punk jazz' or 'no-wave music'. Jackson draws on rhythms from inside and outside jazz.*

CHAPTER FOUR

PAPERWORK

---

6 Standards are tunes that somebody else
wrote, and that was their freedom or their
experience – but then you want to know why
you came on the planet 9

JOANNE BRACKEEN

Jazz composition is often regarded by hard-line fans as a contradiction in terms. On the other hand, listeners attracted by some of the mannerisms of jazz but who dislike the wildness and unpredictability of soloists are inclined to assess the quality of what they hear by how much the players remain 'in the spirit' of what has been written. But the history of jazz has been between these extremes.

The man who developed Scott Joplin's pre-jazz

The Kid from Red Bank – Count Basie turned the jazz band into a vehicle for almost pure rhythm. Long-time partner Freddie Green is in the background.

writing into the beginnings of true jazz composition built around 'sectioning' families of instruments in the band was Jelly Roll Morton. Morton was a colourful and egotistical hustler in turn-of-the-century New Orleans, sometime pimp, entrepreneur, aspirer to the title of World's Greatest Pool Player and a Creole who tried to persuade the world he was white. He learned the piano, and a good deal of music theory, in his teens, and became a successful 'sporting-house' piano player in Storyville. By 1923 he had joined the exodus to Chicago; he recorded a raft of piano solos between 1923 and the end of the Thirties, but made his reputation with recordings under the name Jelly Roll Morton and his Red Hot

Peppers from 1926 to 1930.

Morton's training had given him some understanding of European concert music and the experience led him to use dynamics and mood shifts and a highly imaginative deployment of tone colour in his writing, even with the limited instrumentation. Morton would take the raw materials of New Orleans jazz as exemplified by King Oliver's band, and blend the vocabularies of blues, ragtime and parade music into single compositions.

He brought in extra clarinet players to form the first jazz-band 'reed section'. He would mix episodes of collective improvisation with passages that would reintroduce aspects of the main theme, but played by only one of the instruments over a more restrained and non-contrapuntal accompaniment from the others – repeated figures that amount to the origins of the 'riff'. He would contrast several themes against

each other, or introduce more than one time signature in the same piece. Morton also brought into the repertory rhythms from outside of the New Orleans orbit – the early use of Latin American metres deployed in the tango and the samba. Though Morton died, more or less forgotten, in 1941, he had paved the way for the entire canon of jazz composition.

Meanwhile, a Georgia-born chemistry graduate called Fletcher Henderson was making a most unexpected rise in the music business. Henderson had begun playing piano as a child, and affection for music gradually drew him towards a career in it. Like Ellington, Jimmie Lunceford and Don Redman, Henderson was from the black middle class, such as it was. But racism would have prevented work in the field of American classical music, and these men were drawn to jazz. Their interest coincided with a patronizing, but fast expanding cult status for blacks as 'exotic' nightclub entertainers for white audiences in the Prohibition-era nightclubs of the big northeastern cities; the Kentucky Club and the Cotton Club got big that way.

By a series of accidents and very little purposeful activity (Henderson was a diffident and unambitious man, but he had contacts in the music business through his work as a demo pianist for a record company) a Fletcher Henderson band found itself the main attraction at the Club Alabam in Harlem in 1923. It mostly played pop arrangements, but it included two reed players who were destined for stardom: Don Redman and Coleman Hawkins.

Redman turned out to be a gifted arranger. He began dividing the ensemble into reeds and brass and playing one off against the other. On the tune 'Copenhagen' (1924) on which Louis Armstrong is also featured, Redman has extensively developed the chopping and changing of ensemble playing between the sections, and the technique of writing a basic riff for one group and punctuating it with 'commentary' from another is powerfully audible. These techniques were the foundation stones of arranged jazz for larger ensembles, and Redman more or less pioneered the standard big-band instrumentation. Henderson learned extensively from Redman, but his own work was simpler.

LEFT *Fletcher Henderson – a crucial pioneer in the development of orchestral jazz. Diffident and unambitious, he and his partner Don Redman nevertheless did much*
to found the big-band 'sections' of today.

RIGHT *Don Redman helped transform the early Fletcher Henderson band from a 1920s pop outfit to a pathfinding orchestra.*

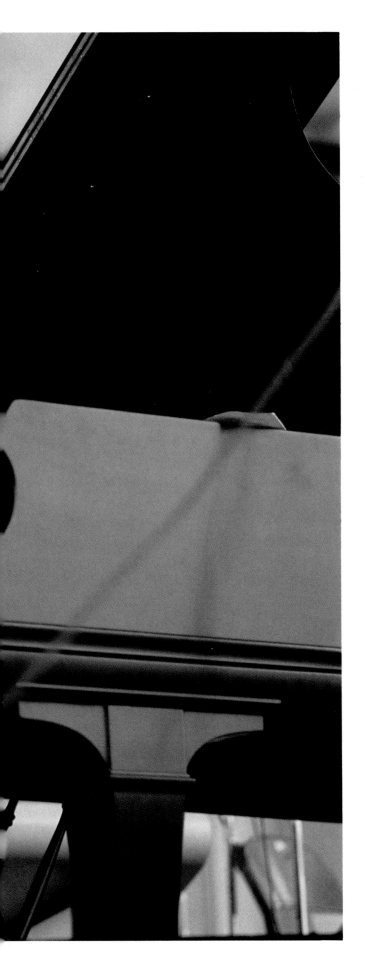

They loved him madly – Duke Ellington, the urbane and farsighted pianist and composer who broke most of the jazz orchestra rules except swing. He gave the big band the breadth of a jazz symphony orchestra.

If Fletcher Henderson was one of the key pioneers of the development of orchestral jazz, the one that became synonymous with jazz music in the minds of fans and non-fans alike was Edward Kennedy 'Duke' Ellington. Ellington's music swung, but the complexity and imagination of it took it out of the orbit of the commercial dance music of the Thirties and Forties and set it in surroundings that the American public was willing to embrace as 'art'.

A Washingtonian, born in 1899, Ellington gained the nickname 'Duke' because he was a sharp dresser from boyhood. His father worked for the U.S. Navy, which gave the family virtually middle class status. By his late teens, having been taught the piano as a child (but with ambitions to be a painter), Ellington was holding down professional jobs around Washington, playing rags and dance music.

Like Fletcher Henderson, Duke Ellington led dance bands early on, with very little jazz content. But by the mid-Twenties, by now working in New York, Ellington had acquired trumpeter James 'Bubber' Miley and saxophonist Sidney Bechet for his band. These two players – Miley with his growling tone and Oliver-like use of mutes, Bechet with his limitless improvisational ingenuity – taught Ellington the fundamentals of jazz. Acquaintance with the King Oliver band in Chicago also contributed to Ellington's growing feeling that the music he was playing lacked something.

Again echoing Henderson, Ellington's band secured a New York job that started the ball rolling for him. A five-year apprenticeship at the Cotton Club – much of it providing backup for the exotic 'jungle' routines so popular with the white punters – turned Ellington from an entertainer into a composer.

Ellington's skills were displayed in the audacity with which he broke the regular jazz-orchestra rules, even early on. The theme of 'Mood Indigo', for instance, combines trumpet, trombone and clarinet, blended into one sound, with the brass instruments muted. He was also a gifted melodist, his understanding of harmony enabling him to break out of the predictable backdrop of swing and situate his music in a world of considerable ambiguity of key. And he constantly wrote pieces that broke the standard 32-bar song form, or the 12 bars of blues. These attributes, put behind some of the finest soloists in jazz, were to produce orchestra performances of a lingering, evocative and frequently rather nostalgic or wistful quality. But all the Ellington bands could tear it up when the time came.

By the 1960s Ellington was writing longer pieces, concerto-like compositions devoted to members of his band. He would use the sound of the soloists – particularly altoist Johnny Hodges, trumpeter Cootie Williams, trombonist Tricky Sam Nanton – as inspirations for compositions, or throw them a fragment of a melody in his head, hear the musicians spontaneously develop it and use this new stage as the basis of a composition.

The Fifties and Sixties saw Ellington become a cultural institution, and he even managed to con-

found listeners who thought that meant he was stagnating by a whirlwind performance at the 1956 Newport Jazz Festival which combined the frenetic drive of a rock concert with the richness that had made him famous. He continued to work into his seventies, and was an ambassador for America's major art form all over the world.

But at the height of the swing craze, Ellington was too subtle to be in the forefront of the public taste. It was Benny Goodman's band that was an emblem of the 'swing age'. Its sound was also heavily dependent fine soloists – trumpeters Bunny Berigan and Cootie Williams, pianist Jess Stacy, guitarist Charlie Christian and the excellent clarinet playing of Goodman himself.

Though orchestra leader Jimmie Lunceford, with the considerable assistance of arranger Sy Oliver, substantially changed the big ensemble sound of jazz from the initial impetus it had had from Henderson, it was the Kansas bands who transformed it. Lunceford developed a smeared, sensuous way of writing for the saxophones that, in a corrupted version, became a model for dance band sax writing thereafter. But it was the Bennie Moten, Count Basie, Jay McShann and Andy Kirk bands of Kansas City that really changed swing.

Kirk's arranger, Mary Lou Williams, was the primary influence in shifting that band's sound from the usual pumping riffs, but it was Basie who paraded the virtues of controlled yet exhilarating swing more triumphantly than anyone else in the idiom, and he went on doing it for 50 years to come. Apart from the emphatic dominance of the riff, in which the sections eventually came to function like a complementary rhythm section, guitarist Freddie Green and drummer Jo Jones laid down a surging, ecstatic beat and Basie himself, a master of understatement and wry, prodding charm at the piano, added much to the ensemble's relaxed appeal. An illustrious succession of bandleaders of the Fifties and onwards used Basie as their inspiration – like Maynard Ferguson, Shorty Rogers, Quincy Jones and Gerry Mulligan.

Ellington had shown an audacious use of tone colours and a willingness to submerge the traditional section divisions beneath the provision of the right texture behind the soloist. This mingled with the riff-driven swing of Basie in the work of Woody Herman. Like Fletcher Henderson, Herman has always treated himself as a modest contributor but a powerful catalyst. His bands grew out of blues-dominated pop orchestras in the 1930s, since Herman took over the band of songwriter Isham Jones in 1936 and maintained it as 'The Band That Plays The Blues' until the formation of his 'First Herd' in 1944.

From that point on, notably with the contributions of arranger Ralph Burns and excellent sidemen including saxophonists Stan Getz and Flip Phillips and trombonist Bill Harris, Herman's work became an increasingly sophisticated blend of orchestral jazz and some devices that bordered on classical borrowings. For instance, Ralph Burns's 'Early Autumn' suite, mentioned earlier, was virtually an orthodox jazz counterpart to Igor Stravinsky's use of some jazz tonalities in a classical setting. Stravinsky wrote a piece in three movements, 'The Ebony Concerto' for Herman's orchestra in 1945, and it remains one of the more successful classical-jazz hybrids. The Herman orchestra survived in various guises until the leader's

The imaginative pianist and arranger Mary Lou Williams, linchpin of Andy Kirk's Kansas swing band in the 1930s, heavily influenced by bebop from the 1950s onward.

on the Fletcher Henderson arrangements and it wasn't until the arrival of Eddie Sauter in the Forties that it acquired a technique that departed from the section-against-section contrasts of the earlier arranger, Sauter beginning to mix dissimilar horns into sections. The Goodman band's early sound was hardly startling, but it was a good showcase for some

death in 1987, its sound progressively altering with the inclusion of electric and pop-music ingredients from the 1960s onwards.

Also on the bridge between jazz and semi-formal music stood Stan Kenton, but Kenton was not simply attracted to musical devices he might borrow from the straight world and fuse with the more small-scale potential of a jazz ensemble. Kenton went for size and bravura, mingled with a strong flavour of the work of French composer Darius Milhaud, with whom the Kenton band's major arranger Pete Rugolo had studied. Kenton added strings and woodwinds and was clearly intent on building a jazz orchestra equal in size and impact to a classical one, bolting on obvious devices purloined from Stravinsky and Bartok where he could.

With the rise of bebop in the 1940s, a new kind of writing for big bands that were still primarily swing-oriented began to be heard. Herman's band bought some pieces from Dizzy Gillespie in the early years of the decade, and they instantly brought a new urgency to the sound of the orchestra, full of packed,

jostling section work and ebullient trumpet parts. The same effect was found in bands led by the pianist Earl Hines and the singer Bill Eckstine in the same period. But it was Dizzy Gillespie himself, picking up many of the members of the disbanding Eckstine outfit and augmenting their work with the Cuban rhythmic effects introduced by percussionist Chano Pozo, who produced the nearest thing to a bebop orchestra. Gillespie had been fascinated by Latin-American idioms since his exposure to the Cuban Machito band.

LEFT *Trumpeter Dizzy Gillespie with his big band. A revolutionary orchestra in the late 1940s, it still delivers thrilling music today.*

However much experimentation might go on within them, jazz orchestras still had a role to play for dancers. The Claude Thornhill Orchestra was almost entirely a dance band, but its lustrous, drifting arrangements and the dissolution of the orthodox sections to release glowing new tone colours, was a significant stepping stone in the development of a departure in jazz writing – although one that had clearly absorbed many of the innovations of Duke Ellington.

Gil Evans was the major architect of this style. Though strongly influenced by Ellington, he was also inclined to the sounds of European orchestral music and in his early arrangements there are few extremes of dynamics, little use of complex or bravura passages for the brass, only the most re-strained and nudging use of riffs, and frequent expansion of the jazz instrumentation with french horns and tubas. These effects were heard in 1949 on the 'Birth of the Cool' recordings with Miles Davis, Lee Konitz, Gerry Mulligan and others. They were

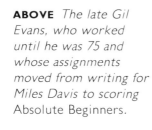

ABOVE *The late Gil Evans, who worked until he was 75 and whose assignments moved from writing for Miles Davis to scoring Absolute Beginners.*

greatly refined by the end of the Fifties when Evans was embroidering lustrous backdrops for Miles Davis's trumpet in classic albums such as 'Porgy and Bess' and 'Sketches of Spain'.

Evans continued to keep an open mind about what constitutes permissible jazz material right into the 1980s, using electronics and rock guitarists, and

working up to his death in March 1988. But the effect never became bludgeoning or histrionic. Like Ellington, Evans continued to use each instrument as if it were a colour on a palette, and his pieces thus vibrate with unexpected sonorities. (He has less of Ellington's devotion to the idea of writing for a particular individual, partly a question of big-band economics.) He also carried to the limits the Ellington idea of composing out of the already-rolling improvisations of the sidemen. Evans's ensemble writing often sounds improvised too, because he leaves the players considerable flexibility to intone it as they wish. A number of excellent composers have appeared from the Evans tributary, notably Zimbabwean-born Michael Gibbs and Canadian trumpeter Kenny Wheeler.

The innovations in jazz writing that followed the 'cool' experiments of 1949 and the voicings developed by Evans were taken up by the baritone saxophonist Gerry Mulligan in small-group forms. Mulligan had written tunes for the 'Birth of the Cool' sessions, notably 'Jeru', 'Rocker' and 'Venus de Milo'. Not long afterwards he was taking this softly spoken but melodically garrulous music further with a tentet of his own that featured the trumpeter Chet

Baker, a man of similar persuasions. Mulligan also formed an unusual piano-less quartet with the delicate Baker in 1952.

Like Gil Evans, George Russell is a modern jazz composer who has continued to be active well into the period of his life at which he earns the double-edged title of 'veteran'. Unlike Evans, who wrote in broad washes of pastel colour shot through with sudden scarlets and purples, Russell is a highly complex composer whose work is founded on studies of alternative scales and shifting key centres he has been developing since the 1950s.

Russell, originally a drummer, came to prominence with compositions (including the famous 'Cubano Be, Cubano Bop') for Dizzy Gillespie's bebop orchestra. His work with his own workshop ensembles in the Fifties and Sixties mingled rearrangements of jazz classics like 'Round Midnight' into his own spiky, angular conception, and originals

LEFT *One of the most advanced theorists in jazz composition – George Russell defies categorization.*

BELOW *The sophistication of Ellington and the roughness and defiance of the ghetto met in Charles Mingus (on bass).*

that frequently sounded like marriages of the most advanced bebop with European conservatory music. Unlike most such blends, however, Russell's affection for jazz came out on top.

Arizona-born bassist Charles Mingus led bands of his own from the early Fifties. Like Russell, they often emerged from 'workshops' in which the new tonalities of bebop were being pushed and pulled into shapes that might lend themselves to composition. Mingus was not sold on the notion of constant tempo throughout a piece, and he was certainly intrigued by bebop's invitation towards new harmony, pushed to the point of dissonance. By 1955 Mingus was developing a repertory company of his own musicians as Ellington had done, and was also deploying Ellington's techniques of programmatic pieces written around particular subjects.

Mingus's music mingled the sophistication of Ellington with the roughness and earthiness of the plantation and railroad origins of jazz. His ensembles frequently shouted and moaned like instrumental representations of old blues players, and he would often work without scores, shouting instructions from the piano and allowing the final form of the piece to emerge in collective improvisation. Into this maelstrom, Mingus would also throw sound effects (car horns were a favourite) and constant stops and starts of tempo. Soloists like the gravelly-toned saxophonist Booker Ervin and the expressive and emotional Eric Dolphy came up through Mingus's bands.

Though Charles Mingus recaptured an earthiness for 'modern' jazz, his technique and that of his musicians was founded on bebop. Booker Ervin in particular, had all the hallmarks of a hard-bop tenorist. Though as we saw earlier hard bop was primarily an improviser's idiom, with only sufficient composition to launch the soloists on their way, the best bands did pay some attention to the charts.

Drummer Art Blakey and pianist Horace Silver founded the famous Jazz Messengers in 1954, and Blakey still leads ensembles by that name today. The style has always been founded on a Basie-like use of riffs and direct, bluesy tunes. Blakey has managed to retain contemporaneity by constantly appointing musical directors to take charge of the arrangements from the ranks of the new arrivals in his band. Lee Morgan and Wayne Shorter both performed this key role for the drummer.

In the early Sixties, the Blakey style began to reflect soul music and funk, an idiom that grew in significance as the Sixties progressed. Blakey's early partner Horace Silver formed several small bands of his own that specialized in this music. Silver was a fine bop pianist, but his percussive attack perfectly suited him for this expository music and his bands were instantly recognizable for themes drawn from gospel and blues, and call-and-response patterns conjuring up the preacher and the congregation. These bands were highly popular and they frequently produced some of the best jazz of the era. But the small groups of the more uncompromising improvisers Clifford Brown and Miles Davis had the edge in depth and range.

A completely different variation of bebop in a band as long-lived as Art Blakey's was that practised by the Modern Jazz Quartet. This began as a showcase for Milt Jackson's vibraphone, and wound up as a sophisticated and highly-wrought vehicle for restrained improvisation within the contexts of European chamber-group devices favoured by its pianist John Lewis. Though the M.J.Q. was often lambasted by jazz critics who disliked its urbanity and eschewing of extremes, it could, however, frequently act as a kind of magnifying glass with which to view the minutiae of musical relationships and it resuscitated collective improvisation in ways that were often both lyrical and swinging.

In 1965 composer and pianist Carla Bley and trumpeter Mike Mantler began composing extensively for the emerging free-improvising players of the period. Bley, a student of George Russell, developed a completely distinctive manner of composition less intricate than Russell's and as luxurious as Gil Evans'. But if Evans's weakness was melody (sometimes his music appears to ebb and flow with textural changes but relying on a soloist to supply melody), Bley is an inspired melodist and her compositions are frequently played, both in orchestral form and by pianists. The appeal of a massive work like the late Sixties' 'Escalator Over the Hill' lies in the conjunction of rich and frequently consonant backdrops for the more abstract solo voices of musicians like Don Cherry and Roswell Rudd.

An ex-Fletcher Henderson sideman Sonny Blount – or Sun Ra – has also claimed an inimitable niche at the free end of jazz composition – not least because his bands are as startling theatrically (musicians in space suits, dancers, ritualistic mimes performed by the leader) as they are musically. Sun Ra believes that he travels through time and space. Whether he does or not, he has – with a distinctly pragmatic imagination – blended the traditional big-band materials of Count Basie and the saxophone sounds of Duke Ellington with influences from Egypt, Africa and early blues.

German free pianist Alex von Schlippenbach uses looser and less idiomatic materials than Sun Ra in his

Carla Bley, a student of George Russell, has written many memorable themes, scored imaginatively for large orchestras, and latterly used much humour and pastiche with her own band.

Globe Unity Orchestra, though it will veer from flat-out, squalling, large-scale jamming to affectionate send-ups of early jazz. The London Jazz Composers' Orchestra, brainchild of the remarkable bassist Barry Guy – a performer as comfortable in conventional classical music as in free jazz – takes its inspiration both from the post-Coltrane-era soloists working in it and modern European compositional devices reminiscent of Penderecki, Berio or Xenakis.

Whether the avant-garde spawned the enthusiasm for jazz-rock fusion that permeated much of the music of the late Sixties and Seventies, or whether it evolved from the increasing use of jam-session performances and prolonged improvisation by rock bands is hard to judge. Both elements were certainly implicated. A track like 'Stuff' from the mid-Sixties Miles Davis album 'Miles in the Sky' reveals techniques that were viewed as heretical by some of Davis's more traditional fans; Herbie Hancock plays an electric piano; Davis's horn squeals into the upper register as if echoing Jimi Hendrix; and drummer Tony Williams plays a ticking, mesmeric rock beat, but without a rock drummer's rambunctious embroidery.

A few years later, Davis was putting his trumpet through wah-wah electronics, batteries of drummers were thundering out tempos a long way from four-four, and the architect of cool jazz was very nearly a rock star. From an arranger's point of view, a startling element in all this is the expansion of the rhythm section to the point where the rhythm virtually replaces the old front line. Davis and his musicians often seemed to be wandering distantly in a forest of seething rhythmic sounds.

A partner of the trumpeter's in this period, the British guitarist John McLaughlin, also began to experiment in his own way with the idiom. The music written for his early Mahavishnu Orchestra was some of the most effective of the era – reflecting both Coltrane's incantatory music and sophisticated use of dynamics and drama. Vibraphonist Gary Burton also began to use the time signatures of the style and harsher, more metallic guitarists, though the writing developed an attractive blend of Bill Evans's lyricism and country music.

But the most musical and resourceful of the fusion bands composed of jazz players investigating rock rather than the other way around, was Weather Report. Founded on a highly creative partnership between pianist Joe Zawinul and saxophonist Wayne Shorter, Weather Report got together in 1971 and lasted with personnel changes into the 1980s. The emphasis was on intelligent and delicate use of the synthesizer to create colourful soundscapes against which acoustic instruments could improvise; considerable textural variation in the percussion; and a ballad-player's lyricism on slow pieces that could

make the entire band sound as effective as a Stan Getz solo – an achievement almost unheard of in the percussive typhoon of most fusion playing.

Guitarist Pat Metheny, as inventive a user of synthesizers as Zawinul, has continued the Weather Report legacy into even more graceful and melodic territory. And in Europe, many musicians have developed versions of the style, though their weaknesses have often been a leaden and colourless rhythmic quality. One of the most impressive – at least in its early incarnations – was Nucleus, a band led by the excellent British trumpeter Ian Carr.

Also in Europe, and using far less intractable materials, there is the Willem Breuker Kollektief, an extraordinary and frequently hilarious ensemble that draws from New Orleans jazz, tangos and waltzes, 1930s big-band bravura, Kurt Weill and post-Sixties free music. Breuker, who emerged from a Dutch school primarily oriented towards free playing, found the exclusion or distortion of traditional methods restrictive. He also missed the opportunity to entertain non-specialized audiences, which his band does with considerable aplomb.

Music with a catholicity quite close to Breuker's has appeared in the increasingly popular repertoires of all-saxophone ensembles. Notable practitioners in this busy, contrapuntal style have been the World Saxophone Quartet, the 29th Street Saxophone Quartet, the Rova Quartet and the British group Itchy Fingers.

The 'sharp end' of an arranged jazz is still being honed by the multi-instrumentalist Anthony Braxton. Composing for non-improvisers as well as improvisers, Braxton frequently expresses his music

TOP RIGHT *Sun Ra on keyboards, a bandleader whose onstage eccentricities disguise an incisive musical mind, blending jazz and Third World musical influences.*

RIGHT *'Great Black Music – Ancient to the Future' – the Art Ensemble of Chicago, personnel unchanged for nearly 20 years, makes beautiful music in every style from New Orleans to 'free-jazz'.*

in graphic or illustrated scores and sometimes titles his pieces with algebraic formulae. And if Braxton operates on the extremes of the intellectualized end of new jazz (though this is a word he would himself wish to avoid), Alice Coltrane operates at an extreme of spiritual or devotional jazz.

Between the two areas comes the doyen of post-Sixties improvising ensembles, the Art Ensemble of Chicago. Featuring a line-up that has remained largely unchanged over 20 years, the outfit (as much inclined to visual display and special effects as Sun Ra) performs work adapted from the entire tradition of jazz: what its members describe as a repertoire of 'Great Black Music – ancient to the future'. Themes will move from jostling forest sounds, the rustling and squawks of animals and birds, to infectiously swinging New Orleans playing or bebop. Owing something to early Mingus, and a lot to the tonal innovations of John Coltrane and Ornette Coleman, an Art Ensemble performance can be an inspirational survey of where the Afro-American music tradition has been and where it may be going.

CHAPTER FIVE

PRECIOUS IVORY

'We in black music think of the piano as a
percussive instrument: we beat the keyboard,
we get inside the instrument'

CECIL TAYLOR

The most popular music in the States around the turn of the century was ragtime. And the most popular instrument was the piano. Many families owned one, children were cajoled or propelled into learning how to play it, and every place of entertainment from the brothel to the theatre depended on one for its music. Though the instrument demanded more of its practitioners than, say, a saxophone, it was commonly played (and often very proficiently) by those who had only the most rudimentary knowledge of

Errol Garner, a pianist with a beat like a big band, and a composer of enduring tunes, including the famous 'Misty'.

what a standard European piano education entailed. Nevertheless, it was difficult to be even a self-taught pianist without having a more sophisticated harmonic awareness than a self-taught wind-player: the architecture of harmony was laid out before you in neat rows. Even the early pianists were able to give jazz a 'vertical' subtlety that was more advanced than the hit-and-miss counterpoint of much New Orleans music. The problem for piano players who wanted to play jazz was simply that a note struck on a keyboard is very different to a note blown on a horn. It's hard to bend or distort or 'vocalize' its sound in a way that was soon recognized as a cornerstone of jazz music's expressiveness, and pianists had to find other ways around this serious obstacle.

The early pianists primarily devoted themselves to ragtime – a relative of jazz but not interchangeable with it – and they were self-contained soloists who needed to collaborate with no one. They played for dancers, and their repertoire, in addition to rags, consisted of pop songs, waltzes, foxtrots, square dances, music hall hits and anything else that would qualify as musically fashionable in the early years of the 20th century.

Predominantly northerners, they were unfamiliar with blues, and they worked in parts of the States as yet unfamiliar with what the migrating jazz musicians of the southlands were to bring with them. The stamping grounds of musicians like Eubie Blake, James P. Johnson, Luckyeth Roberts and Willie 'The Lion' Smith were the northeastern cities. Johnson, from New Jersey, worked predominantly in Harlem (he was one of the first blacks to record a piano roll) and he was as likely to throw into his recitals quotes from Beethoven or Liszt as he was to play Scott Joplin. So were most of the principal figures of the 'Harlem stride school'.

As they began to hear the early jazz, their first transformations of piano style involved the rhythmic changes that the New Orleans musicians had already set rolling – principally to dislocate the melody from the dictatorship of the beat. The left hand playing of these pianists is almost pure ragtime. The right is predominantly chordal, but full of embellishment and trills. It was not an accompanist's style, or even a soloist's within a band. It was a world of its own, even after the first incursions of jazz.

Thomas 'Fats' Waller shot to fame out of the Harlem stride group. The son of a preacher, he was taught piano for a while as a child but preferred ragtime to hymns. As a teenager he was drawn into the black cabaret and entertainment world around 125th Street. James P. Johnson was impressed by him, and gave him lessons.

By the beginning of the 1920s, Waller's talents had blossomed so much that he was making piano rolls, turning out streams of compositions, and within ten years he was almost as hot a showbusiness property as Louis Armstrong. Waller died in 1943, his health wrecked by drink and gluttony, and his musical legacy is generally regarded as an effortlessly amiable repertoire of memorable tunes ('Honeysuckle Rose', 'Rosetta'), novelty songs and comedian's patter. But on both piano and organ – an instrument he loved – he was surprisingly thoughtful and musically rich.

Meanwhile, a long way from Harlem, another piano style was being mobilized. The blues playing of the South wouldn't have taxed the skills of a trained pianist much but it lay at the limit of what was possible for self-taught players, many of whom were still cotton-pickers or railroad labourers themselves.

It revolved around repeated, highly rhythmic bass figures with fragmentary, single-line melodies in the right hand – often sliding a black note into a white one to create the horn-like effect of a blue or bent note. The style was called 'boogie-woogie', and it had much more in common with the early jazz.

Something like it had probably been played by rudimentary pianists in the South for a half a century before jazz was born. When there was considerable interest in blues players in the 1920s – before the Depression contributed to the demise of blues as a hot property for record companies – some of the part-time musicians who played in this style managed to get on to disc. Jimmy Yancey, Roosevelt Sykes and Cow Cow Davenport were amongst them. The style went out of favour in the Thirties but resurfaced at the end of the decade – so much so that many swing bands included a boogie tune in their repertoire.

ABOVE *Thomas 'Fats' Waller, the preacher's son who became a pop star of the 1930s. Waller's playing was vivacious and exuberant on piano or organ.*

RIGHT *Pioneering ragtime pianist Eubie Blake, who died in 1983 at the age of 100 and declared 'If I'd known I was going to live this long I'd have taken better care of myself.'*

Meade Lux Lewis, Albert Ammons and Pete Johnson came to the fore in the revival.

With the stride style and boogie-woogie dominating jazz piano in such different ways, it was inevitable that a genius would emerge who could unite them. That man was Earl 'Fatha' Hines.

Hines was born in 1905 in Pittsburgh. His father was a trumpeter and his mother a pianist. Odd music jobs around Pittsburgh in his teens, not apparently discouraged by his family, led to his migration to Chicago in 1923, just as the New Orleans musicians were winding up there. He was already a strong,

two-handed player and exhibited a highly rhythmic manner of playing that attacked the music hard. His talents found him quickly in the company of clarinettist Jimmie Noone and others.

In 1928, Hines replaced Lil Hardin Armstrong in Louis Armstrong's band, and the pianist and trumpeter recorded some startling collaborations. The most celebrated of these was probably 'Weather Bird', an unaccompanied duet. Here Hines's 'trumpet style' is strongly in evidence and his independence from Armstrong's line and yet his constant rhythmic support for it is as sensitive as if the trumpeter

LEFT *Earl Hines – a 'stride' player with a strong flavour of the blues and a bold, robust attack.*

BELOW LEFT *Teddy Wilson was urbane and elegant where Hines was flushed and vigorous. He made a perfect foil for Benny Goodman's soaring clarinet.*

BELOW RIGHT *The man who wrote his own rulebook for jazz piano. Art Tatum possessed a technique that classical virtuoso Vladimir Horowitz marvelled at. Though accused at times of substituting embroidery for substance, Tatum's harmonic insights made his pieces constant sources of surprise.*

niments. Wilson joined Benny Carter's band in 1933, an ensemble pretty much in his own image, and then Benny Goodman.

The stride school bred another descendant, but one so majestically talented, and equipped so early on in his musical life to proceed in a direction of his own, that he can hardly be conceived of as a member of a school at all. That towering figure of jazz piano is Art Tatum.

Born in Toledo, Ohio, in 1910, blind in one eye and with limited vision in the other, Tatum learned music in a school for the blind, then graduated to the Toledo School of Music. By the time he was in his early teens he was playing at rent parties, and when he was 17 he had his own show on a local radio station, which began to be networked nationwide on the strength of the prodigy's contribution.

Tatum always acclaimed Fats Waller as his inspiration, but he treated his materials more cavalierly than Walther. He would frequently alter the harmonic pattern by substituting chords of his own, regularly career off into different keys and return by the most unexpected routes – in other words, he was improvising not simply remarkably convoluted and original melody lines but the chords as well. What was striking was that these effects, though they did occasionally sound like a superhuman party trick, for the most part remained in sympathy with the original materials, and at the end of his exhausting forays Tatum would return to them without a hitch.

On a purely athletic level, Tatum's improvisations have been timed as running at something like a thousand notes a minute, and simply as a technician he has commanded respect – the kind of respect that brought classical pianists like Gieseking and Horowitz to the unlikely surroundings of New York jazz clubs in the Thirties. Horowitz apparently listened to Tatum's rendition of 'Tiger Rag' and said, 'It can't be true. I don't believe my eyes and my ears.'

Of the two piano players who came to the fore after the arrival of bop, one belonged intimately to the new idiom and was conspicuously a technician; the other did not belong to it and did his best to hide the technique. The former was Earl 'Bud' Powell, the latter Thelonious Monk.

Powell, a New Yorker by birth, was 17 when the meetings at Minton's were forging the working materials of bebop. He had been classically trained, but his jazz style was, not surprisingly, heavily influenced by Teddy Wilson. Possessed of a good technique, and operating in a manner that already put a great deal of emphasis on the melodic wanderings of the right hand, Powell's fascination with the beboppers took the form of using that fast right hand to copy Charlie Parker's tumbling horn lines.

But what was also noticeable about the sound of

represented a third hand.

The reason why Hines's piano playing is called 'the trumpet style' is because his right hand – instead of concentrating on the chordal flamboyances and arpeggios of the stride players – plays a good deal of stubby, single-line melody. He varies this with broken phrasing, sudden interruptions of the bass line, cross rhythms and all kinds of departures from the steady flow of music that might have been expected of a musician of his background. This was a lineage that came direct from the early blues players. The mixture of interests made Hines a fulcrum for the maturing of jazz piano.

The Hines style inevitably bred imitators. A black Texan, Teddy Wilson, was one of the most independent, and deservedly celebrated. Highly trained, and highly elegant, Wilson was the most stylish exponent of the idiom in the 1930s. His style was more seamless, less tangential and dramatic than Hines's, and his bass figures were often understated, a soft, padding sound against Hines's thunderous accompa-

LEFT Bud Powell, an architect of modern jazz piano, who took Charlie Parker's saxophone innovations and adapted them for the keyboard.

BELOW A walking definition of 1950s hipsterism (and the originator of an utterly personal keyboard language that the public took some years to catch up with),

Thelonious Monk's style was jarring, dissonant, full of spaces and as percussive as a drummer.

RIGHT Stan Tracey, one of the finest of all British jazz musicians. On the periphery of the 'Monk school', Tracey's style is nevertheless busier, more mischievous and utterly personal.

jazz piano under the influence of bebop was that the plush, orchestral left hand was beginning to shrivel into disuse. The beboppers were experimenting so extensively with harmonic variations, often on the wing, that too explicit a background statement by a harmony instrument could wind up being more of a hindrance than a help.

But if Bud Powell was the spearhead of bop piano whose star steadily waned from dazzling beginnings, the career of Thelonious Monk went the other way, as did his technical and musical inclinations.

Monk, a North Carolina-born self-taught musician who had grown up in New York, was ten years younger than Art Tatum. His early work probably absorbed as much as he could handle of the maestro's right hand style, with a rhythmic approach based on Earl Hines. If these influences made Monk a stride pianist who happened to have thrown in his lot with the boppers, that's what he was. But he was a very unusual kind of stride pianist.

Whitney Balliett once immortally described Monk's piano phrasing as resembling somebody 'missing the bottom step in the dark'. His timing was eccentric, a mixture of sudden spurts of sound (often including a fractured, stabbing dissonance) and long silences. He didn't always follow the bebop trademark of switching the accents from the swing-based one-and-three to the 'modern' two-and-four. He was as much inclined as the other beboppers to use augmented or unusual components of a harmony, but instead of incorporating them smoothly into a run, he would forcibly – and often jarringly – emphasize them as if to ensure that listeners could not miss what was being done. Even the bebop pioneers didn't always welcome Monk's fierce independence.

For most of the 1950s Monk remained in relative obscurity – despite some stunning recordings, in-

cluding the famous 'Brilliant Corners', which displayed both his writing and improvising quirkiness. It wasn't until a remarkable collaboration between Monk and John Coltrane which took place at New York's Five Spot in 1957 that the pianist came to receive some of the public encouragement that should have been his since the Forties.

Monk didn't really breed imitators because his methods were so wayward – but some musicians have taken a lead from him, notably Randy Weston, Herbie Nichols and Mal Waldron among Americans, Stan Tracey in Britain , and Misja Mengelberg (who later became absorbed by free playing) in Holland. Nichols has belatedly come to be recognized as a composer of almost as compelling a quirkiness and originality as Monk, but this recognition did not come soon enough to make the pianist's life any easier. Waldron – a one-time accompanist of Billie Holiday – plays in an instantly recognizable percussive, even glowering manner, his improvising never far away from firmly planted block chords.

Tatum also was a hard act to follow, though the Canadian pianist Oscar Peterson has gone a long way towards repeating it, with a style as breathless, as preoccupied with fast tempos, and generally dripping with almost as much jewellery as Tatum's. So has the Polish pianist Adam Makowicz. West Indian pianist Monty Alexander has joined the Tatum line through the influence of Peterson.

Errol Garner, a self-taught musician who arrived on the New York jazz scene in the 1940s, went on to enjoy a considerable popular reputation as a jazz pianist who was highly inventive yet possessed of a steady supply of hummable tunes. Garner's style was founded in swing, and plush, romantic, orchestral improvising flooded from him. It was always engagingly underpinned by a powerful, percussive left hand, however – even if the pianist's cascading introductions and sly but endlessly postponed insinuations of the theme tantalizingly delayed the eruption of the 'Garner beat'. Inability to read music didn't stop him from composing some memorable songs – the most enduring being 'Misty', a staple in his own repertoire and in that of many other musicians.

Another popular swing pianist to have founded a career on the Hines-Wilson-Tatum school was the Englishman George Shearing, a blind musician who emigrated to the States after the Second World War. Though Shearing's background was in swing, and one of his significant influences was the two-handed block-chord style of Milt Buckner, he incorporated a good deal of bebop into his music after his arrival in America. Much of his work,however, blended into M.O.R. and he downplayed his improvisatory skills to broaden his appeal.

Another pianist with allegiances to several schools of piano playing at once is Dave Brubeck. For a while

Brubeck enjoyed as much commercial success as jazz musicians could ever have expected to achieve; his group was one of the biggest draws on the concert circuit at the end of the 1950s. Brubeck became famous for his experiments with rhythm – aided by a remarkable drummer, Joe Morello – but his eclecticism came from a musical background that included the influence of Bach and Darius Milhaud as much as swing. Brubeck's style depends on clanging chords and dramatic – some would say overblown – crescendos. His partnership with saxophonist Paul Desmond, however, frequently produced excellent jazz.

Meanwhile, Jaki Byard, one-time Mingus sideman and originally a swing pianist, has been steadily gathering an enthusiastic following for his much more humorous and exuberant blends of the techniques of Waller, Tatum, Powell and even the boogie-woogie pianists.

An equally resourceful performer with a command of both bebop and the 'orchestral' style but who builds the folk songs of his native Catalonia into his work is the Spaniard Tete Montoliu.

A pianist with a foot in the bebop camp but with an independence that makes him hard to classify except in terms of his own standards is Lennie Tristano. He was a classically trained musician who literally founded his own 'school' of jazz at the end of the Forties. His jazz was based on an ambiguous, loosely structured kind of improvisation and a melodic style reminiscent of the cool, mathematical poise of Bach.

The Tristano school players, whatever instrument they played, specialized in long, looping improvised lines that rode over the bar structures or obliterated them altogether. (Tristano further tried to banish the effects of bar-lines by insisting that his drummers and bassists played in as nearly neutral a timekeeping role as possible, suppressing all accents.)

But the pianist of the Forties who most imaginatively grasped the possibilities of bebop piano as married to a richer and more colourful left hand technique was the New Jersey pianist Bill Evans.

Evans was born in 1929, trained on piano, violin and flute as a child, and his first contact with jazz piano was swing. But he left New York when bebop was on the way up, enrolling in the Southeastern Louisiana College, and was subsequently even further distanced from the hothouse of the new music by being enlisted into the army. By the mid-Fifties though, Evans was getting regular jazz work in New York. Given the opportunity to record by the jazz enthusiasts' label, Riverside, he came to the notice of Miles Davis.

Though Evans's tenure with Davis only lasted eight months – he quit because he maintained the experience was exhausting him – it was during those months that 'Kind of Blue' was made. Evans's playing on that album – ruminative, trembling with evaporating arpeggios, sometimes unexpectedly shot through with steely single-line figures from which it would begin to pulse with rhythm – was a cornerstone of its success and contributed much to the displaced and ambiguous quality that eventually made it such a modern jazz landmark.

Evans's pensiveness has sometimes been criticized as a weakness. Though it is the predominant mood of his playing, he was always able to swing hard on

LEFT *Dave Brubeck, a musically cultivated and eclectic performer who has specialized in daunting time signatures, classical hybrids and a dramatic, climactic style.*

RIGHT *A great piano improvisor in a manner mostly pensive, but fitfully erupting into a restless swing, Bill Evans influenced pianists like Keith Jarrett and Herbie Hancock.*

BELOW *Jaki Byard, a one-time partner of Charles Mingus, is one of the best-equipped of all jazz pianists, able to switch from stride piano to bebop and beyond without turning a hair. His playing sometimes resembles an exuberant history lesson in the art.*

ABOVE *Herbie Hancock and Chick Corea in concert.*

LEFT *McCoy Tyner's style evolved as a pianistic equivalent to the work of his most famous boss, John Coltrane.*

RIGHT *Usually heard as an unaccompanied pianist, Keith Jarrett's music is a rich blend of jazz, gospel and country-and-western. He also composes semi-classical scores and has lately returned to reinterpreting jazz standards.*

uptempo tunes when he needed to. In this guise his music took on a restlessly shifting short-phrase urgency. Frequently deploying the device of repeating figures of roughly similar patterns in different registers, it gave an impression of darting, glittering mobility.

Though there have also been further descendants of the Bud Powell school, like Wynton Kelly, some musicians have combined that tradition with a bluesier or more gospel-like strain. Bobby Timmons and Hampton Hawes have fitted into this category, with Ramsey Lewis the most commercial exponent of the idiom.

But for all these high-class keyboard artists, Bill Evans was unquestionably one of the most influential pianists on the jazz scene of the 1960s. Many musicians who have gone on to build reputations if anything bigger than his, began as close attendants on his style. Among these are Herbie Hancock, Keith Jarrett, Chick Corea, and to some extent McCoy Tyner, although Tyner was as powerfully influenced by his most famous employer, John Coltrane.

Hancock was a child prodigy, performing Mozart with the Chicago Symphony Orchestra when he was 11. He had an illustrious career as a Blue Note recording artist in the early Sixties, working with older players like Dexter Gordon, and indicating his preferences for a blend of bop and early funk – the latter led to a hit composition, 'Watermelon Man'.

As a sideman with Miles Davis, Hancock demonstrated a mixture of displaced, porous chords and Bill Evans–like melodic ambiguity that contained volumes more in the way of musicality than the commercial sallies into funk he has frequently embarked on since.

Keith Jarrett, born in Pennsylvania in 1945, has shared much of Hancock's background but never ventured into funk. Much of his work now consists of solo recitals in formal concert halls, or semi-classical compositions. As an improviser, however, though he's prone to verbosity and a kind of glitzy sentimentality at times, Jarrett can be hypnotic. He exhibits the sensitivity and delicacy of Bill Evans, but often combines it with a chiming, song-like backdrop that frequently resembles country and western music. His playing may display anything from baroque music to boogie or gospel, and rarely abandons a steady, mesmerizing left-hand rhythm. Lately, Jarrett has been releasing albums of jazz standards featuring himself with a trio, in which his descent from Bill Evans is clearly, but creatively, displayed.

Armando 'Chick' Corea is the third of the pianists who came up through the Miles Davis bands of the 1960s and helped put the keyboard back on the map of public perceptions through a good deal of conspicuous commercial work. Like Hancock,

Corea is a student both of bebop and the classical traditions. He also often echoes Evans, but has a more flamboyant tendency to display borrowings from Debussy or Ravel, as well as an enduring enthusiasm for Latin music. Like Hancock, he has also essayed into funk and jazz-rock – but fairly predictably.

Evans's other illustrious offspring, McCoy Tyner, has never dabbled in pop music. He has spent his playing life since he left the Coltrane band in the mid-Sixties performing a more accessible and less trance-like version of the music he made alongside Coltrane. This is a highly rhythmic and intense modal style based on furiously storming chords (often two-handed), torrential arpeggios, riffs, and simple, soulful themes, heavily dependent on repetition. But Tyner can handle standards too, even if his tendency is to boil everything in the pressure-cooker of his unrelenting imagination. Tyner's own offspring have included John Hicks, Hilton Ruiz, Englishman John Taylor and the highly imaginative Joanne Brackeen.

If jazz pianists have found it difficult to develop ways of playing that complement the bent notes, distortions and vocalized 'colouring' of the wind instruments, they found the going even harder with the rise of the avant-garde of the late 1950s. The role of a chordal instrument was even more an occasion for suspicion than it was in the era of bebop – which, after all, even if its soloists wanted to break the rules, was still a music with an orthodox harmonic base. The musician who found an answer – such a compelling one that he is sometimes regarded as a more substantial founder of the movement than Ornette Coleman or John Coltrane – is Cecil Taylor.

Taylor is sometimes conveniently summarized as being the possessor of a style more reminiscent of drums than piano. He has also been called 'the Art Tatum of the avant-garde'. Blowing between these two comparisons is a whirlwind technique that blends melodic ideas from Bartok, Stravinsky and Messiaen with those of Duke Ellington and Bud Powell, and featuring blues configurations and even snatches of a boogie left hand.

Taylor's sound is dense and his stamina unquenchable, so the effect of all this beachcombing of musical ideas is that when they can be heard in Taylor's music, they seem to be jostling with each other and whistling past like an express train passing through a station. Taylor began in swing bands but by 1957 (when he appeared in his own right at the Newport Jazz Festival) had formed the basis of his own style. He thus predated the public experimentations of Ornette Coleman and John Coltrane.

Taylor has spawned a variety of followers on the free scene – like Don Pullen, Anthony Davis, Muhal Richard Abrams, powerful British players like Howard Riley and Keith Tippett, German Alex von

Schlippenbach and the Swiss Irene Schweitzer. There have also been gentler exponents of a more reflective kind of 'free' piano, notably Canadian Paul Bley and American Ran Blake. Bley has blended some of the lessons of Cecil Taylor with the moody reflectiveness of Bill Evans, and Blake is a devotee of Thelonious Monk.

As jazz becomes an increasingly international language, pianists have also expanded the sound of the instrument by blending elements from the Afro-American tradition with local ones. Abdullah Ibrahim (formerly known as Dollar Brand) has resoundingly achieved this, working in a style derived originally from Duke Ellington's and Thelonious Monk's but heavily inflected with the chanting, dancing, communal spirit of the music of the South African townships he was born among. Andrew Hill, from Haiti, has combined his own experience of African transplantations with a profound familiarity with European formal music.

LEFT *The self-taught and highly original Joanne Brackeen.*

ABOVE *Cecil Taylor, once called the Art Tatum of the avant-garde, an alchemist of post-bop and modern classical piano materials. With Ornette Coleman and John Coltrane, Taylor's name is intimately associated with the birth of 'free-jazz'.*

RIGHT *Abdullah Ibrahim, formerly Dollar Brand, the Ellington-influenced South African pianist.*

CHAPTER SIX

WAY
DOWN
LOW

> ❛ A bass is about time, and sound. If you
> want to play fast, play a guitar ❜

DANNY THOMPSON, BRITISH BASS PLAYER

If George 'Pops' Foster – who worked with King Oliver, Kid Ory and many others – was the first great name in jazz bass, Jimmy Blanton was the hero of the pre-modern era – and like guitarist Charlie Christian, a very short-lived one. No one had seriously thought of making the bass an independent solo voice before him. Tuberculosis killed Blanton in 1942 when he was 21, but even by this time it was evident that two years of astonishing work with Duke Ellington had liberated the string bass in jazz forever.

George 'Pops' Foster, who worked with all the early jazz legends, including King Oliver, Sidney Bechet and Louis Armstrong.

Where Pops Foster and later the swing bassists like John Kirby and Walter Page had contented themselves with a solid, dependable rhythmic line beneath the soloists, Blanton had not allowed himself to believe the conventional wisdom about how inflexible or awkward a double bass inevitably had to be. Blanton invented ways of playing it that were completely fresh, developing a contrapuntal technique that made it possible for a completely independent yet complementary melody line to be played against the horns.

Blanton was a violinist originally, having studied the instrument with an uncle. He took up the bass at Tennessee State College and began playing with local bands and student bands at that time. He had joined Fate Marable's band on riverboat trips in 1937, and was spotted by Duke Ellington in St. Louis, and signed at once. Where Pops Foster had been solid, reliable, a rock, Blanton started to play the bass as if it were a horn in the agility of its melodies, and like a guitar in the range of its effects. Where earlier bassists had played one-note-to-the-beat walking rhythms based on the notes of each chord, Blanton would play much more complicated figures than these. His tone had a lightness and expressiveness that had never been achieved on the rather smudgy-sounding instrument before and his timekeeping was immaculate.

Notably, he developed the use of the 'double stop'

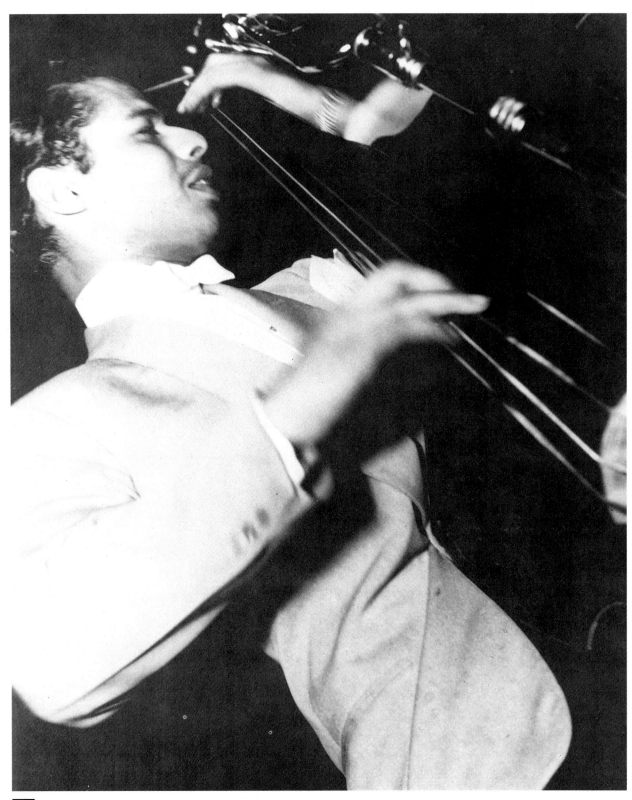

– sounding two strings of the instrument simultaneously – and also used much smaller subdivisions of the beat to vary the accents on the rhythm, much as the more advanced drummers were doing at the same time. Blanton lifted the Ellington orchestra to its greatest heights during this period, and ended the phase in which some critics had found the only significant fault with the band to be its unexciting rhythm playing. Blanton left the orchestra in 1941 as his tuberculosis took its toll of him, and died the following year.

Following Blanton came Oscar Pettiford, Ray Brown and Charles Mingus. Pettiford, like Blanton, had startling control of melodic variation and tone, and his construction of solos – small masterpieces of balance and expressiveness – was as generous a tribute to Blanton as could have been conceived. Like many American jazz musicians in the 1950s, Pettiford left for Europe, and died in Copenhagen in 1960.

Blanton's innovations had been perfect for bebop. Not all the early bebop bassists – including those who appear on some of the most enduring of early bop recordings – were in the same league as the major front-line soloists, but Ray Brown is certainly one who was. Brown's grasp of bop fundamentals and ability to improvise with them was so unusual that Dizzy Gillespie's big band even made part of their repertoire a feature for Brown entitled 'One Bass Hit'. When the impresario Norman Granz sought to recreate the Ellington/Blanton duets of the early war years, it was Brown he asked to be Ellington's partner, and the tribute was resoundingly successful on 'This One's For Blanton'. Brown has continued to exemplify the undemonstrative but subtle gifts of the technically assured double bass player whose work is at the same time entirely at the service of the band and the proceedings. As pianist Oscar Peterson's partner for many years, Brown was virtually the definition

LEFT *Though Jimmy Blanton died at 21, he had already sparked a double-bass revolution. He offered a counterpoint to the soloists.*

BELOW *Charles Mingus' bass playing had a fierce, preacher-like intensity and his sound boomed like a church-organ. Many tried to imitate him.*

of fleet, flexible, relaxed and infectiously swinging accompaniment.

'Relaxation' would not normally be a quality instantly associated with the late Charles Mingus, but he certainly possessed it musically, and in addition to all the other virtues of the first post-Blanton generation, Mingus was a man of fierce commitment, at times almost frantic energy and a sweeping musical imagination that made him not only the foremost bass player of his generation but one of the finest composers and arrangers as well.

Mingus's technique enabled him to enhance the jazz pizzicato to the point where his continuous plucking of a single note virtually took on the quality of a sustained 'blown' sound. But he also freed himself from the dull and ill-defined sound of much plucked bass with a technique that enabled him to articulate a single note with a percussive sharpness. *New Yorker* critic Whitney Balliett described Mingus's opening choruses on his 1957 'Haitian Fight Song' as easily rivalling Louis Armstrong's opening of 'West End Blues'.

Mingus had a distinctly mixed baptism in music, which contributed to the immense variety and resourcefulness of his playing. He played in a traditional New Orleans band led by the then veteran Kid Ory in the 1940s; he played with Lionel Hampton towards the end of that decade, and then in a trio with the vibraphone player Red Norvo.

In developing his own music from the 1950s on, Mingus pursued the path that his own bass playing technique had laid open for him – a way of combining the earthiness and directness of the earliest jazz and blues playing with the speed and complexity of bebop. Ellington had turned the relatively meagre orchestral resources of New Orleans and early swing into the raw material for orchestral music of concerto-like impact. Mingus took that tradition and used it in a context in which the whole band would be the soloist. His own bass playing was crucially significant in preventing this potentially chaotic chemical reaction from running amok.

The Mingus generation produced a number of other remarkable bass players who, unsurprisingly, had far more localized impact. Percy Heath, a light-toned bassist with a delicate, almost playful style, perfectly suited the ornate and fragile music of the Modern Jazz Quartet. Leroy Vinnegar and Curtis Counce were two prominent and inventive West Coast bassists in the era of the 'cool school'. Paul Chambers, who worked with many of the principal hard bop players, was a performer whose phrasing was grounded in that combination of gravelly, laconic brusqueness and sudden legato volubility that characterized late bebop. Another powerful bassist of the same school was Wilbur Ware, who held down the demanding job of being a long-term accompanist

ABOVE *A Mingus descendant who achieved both the master's solidity and weight, and developed a voice of his own. Charlie Haden has been long associated with Ornette Coleman.*

RIGHT *Dave Holland is a British musician who went to the States at the behest of Miles Davis. He combines a LaFaro-like dexterity with some of the tone and clout of Mingus, and is also an original writer.*

to the intractable Thelonious Monk. Others in that circle included Jimmy Woode, Wilbur Little, Doug Watkins and Reggie Workman.

Although it might have seemed that Jimmy Blanton had more or less written the book on possible developments for double bass players, two musicians of very different persuasions took matters startlingly further on in the late Fifties. These men were Charlie Haden and Scott LaFaro, the first performing for most of the period with the iconoclastic Ornette Coleman, the second with a piano-player of Chopin-like gracefulness, Bill Evans.

In performing with Coleman, Haden quickly found that the Blanton bass legacy was only going to provide limited guidance. Coleman, though his music retained a swinging pulse and its phrasing was strongly derived from the blues, was not interested in

bebop's refinement of the old music-business song-books, however cleverly it was done. Consequently, a style of bass playing that depended on counterpoint to a top line, or even on all manner of rhythmic variations and embroidery of the bass line with triplets and passing notes, would be of restricted use if there were no regular and repeated chord pattern to the tune.

Coleman issued a chillingly vague instruction to Haden: 'Forget about the changes in key and just play within the range of the idea.' The bassist thus evolved a way of moving in and out of range of the saxophone, sometimes reinforcing whatever knot of melodic ideas Coleman seemed preoccupied by,

sometimes moving away from it and creating a sense of space and openness in the music.

Haden's own solos were frequently Spanish tinged, and strummed like an Andalucian guitarist. This influence came even further to the fore with him when he became a bandleader in his own right for the first exploits of the Liberation Music Orchestra, which used a good deal of Spanish Civil War material in its early stages. Haden is also distinguished by the reverberating vibrato in his sound and his capacity to sound impassioned and stimulated even in the space of a single prolonged note.

If Haden's sound was weighty, unhurried, rich and tremulous, Scott LaFaro's was fast, restless, possessed of a mosquito-like busyness. Like Blanton, LaFaro was another bass genius whose career was cut tragically short (LaFaro died in a car crash in 1961, when he was 25).

LaFaro was a perfect foil for Bill Evans, whom he joined in 1959. The bassist lowered the bridge of his instrument to bring the strings closer to the fingerboard, as a way of increasing the speed with which the instrument could be played. LaFaro was not interested in the role of timekeeper, though he was capable of playing it with almost languid ease. But in collaboration with a pianist possessed of such a driving sense of time as Evans, LaFaro was able to improvise increasingly complex counter-melodies.

Such was the understanding between them that on some of their collaborations (like 'Solar' on the 'Village Vanguard' sessions) the two of them kept together while appearing at times to be engaged on completely separate trains of thought; and at other times they were so intertwined on the same melodic idea that the sound was of one instrument.

As has often been remarked of LaFaro, his solo lines have a guitar-like dexterity and range – the top end of the bass didn't frighten him. It was uncommon to hear a regular 'walking' bass figure when LaFaro was behind Evans, but so intense was their collaboration and so communicative their drive that it wasn't missed.

Two other bassists, Jimmy Garrison and David Izenzon, used guitar-like sounds in their playing, and both men were significant figures in the avant-garde of the Sixties. Garrison played with John Coltrane, joining his ground-breaking band in 1961. At this point Coltrane was exploring a different landscape of the avant-garde to Ornette Coleman, and one that had developed more obviously from the harmonic principles that had gone before.

But Coltrane was exploring polytonality, or the art of playing in two keys at the same time – a familiar development in 20th century concert music, but unfamiliar to most listeners to jazz who had been reared on derivations of the song form. This way of playing, though it developed out of hard bop, required a different way of articulating the bass to the 'walking' rhythm, not least because Coltrane's band included drummer Elvin Jones. Jones was himself altering the basis of rhythmic playing by diverting the 'focus' of the beat from the hi-hat or ride cymbal to a constantly shifting kaleidoscope of patterns so that the 'beat' would be moving from one part of the drumkit to another.

Garrison's most characteristic contribution to the art was a strumming of chords in solos, and sometimes in ensemble, that suggested a flamenco guitar. A musician of a similar persuasion was the academically trained David Izenzon, who performed with Ornette Coleman's bands in the mid-Sixties. Izenzon

used the bow as frequently as he played pizzicato, and was capable of delivering an unbroken solo-like tapestry that acted as the Jackson Pollock-like backdrop to Coleman's audacious forays.

By the beginning of the Seventies, therefore, the vocabulary of the bass had a variety and richness that listeners and practitioners of the instrument could never have conceived 30 years before. The schools of

rhythmic regularity, horn-like virtuosity, contrapuntal and free playing were all thoroughly developed. To this diverse collection came the electric bass guitar and styles of playing that needed to be adapted to the return of two-beat – jazz-funk.

Some musicians – like the British bassist Dave Holland – were adept in all fields. Holland has a

LEFT *Steve Swallow, a purveyor of song-like bass lines.*

BELOW RIGHT *German bassist Eberhard Weber uses electric instruments specially built for him.*

BELOW *A mixture of Motown and jazz guitarist Wes Montgomery, the late Jaco Pastorius transformed what was possible on bass guitar. He frequently played with Weather Report.*

with very dominant percussion sounds, the electric bass – which had been used in rock music since the late Fifties – came to jazz. The problems of adapting it were considerable. It usually sounded muddy and dull, and though it could be played with the agility of a guitar, the tonal qualities of the instrument killed most of the drive and attack that very fast pizzicato playing could produce on the upright instrument.

Steve Swallow effectively used the electric bass from early on, and developed a highly musical, singing tone with it – partly because his phrasing always sounded deceptively simple, like somebody humming a tune. But it was the merging of the Motown bassists' vigorous thumbing technique, Scott LaFaro's lightning phrasing, and guitarist Wes Montgomery's style of soloing in octaves that revolutionized the instrument in the hands of Jaco Pastorius. Pastorius was killed in an incident at a club in 1987.

LaFaro-like virtuosity at speed and in pitch and tempo, but he can also play without formal structures and much of his apprenticeship in England was performed with free-improvising ensembles before he joined the Miles Davis band and his career was transformed by emigration to the States. Another ex-Miles Davis performer of startling technique, though not much enthusiasm for the free scene, is Ron Carter.

Carter is now 51, a Michigan-born musician who studied cello originally but moved over to jazz because he thought that the opportunities for black classical players might be limited. If anything, Carter has continued the apparently exhausted task of refining the violin- or guitar-like agility of modern bassists still further. No tempo can unbalance him and the notes seem to skip and dance from his instrument.

With fusion music played at high volume, and

The voice of the bass is now so transformed that concerts featuring the solo instrument are no longer an oddity. German bassist Eberhard Weber frequently does this, playing in conjunction with electronic synthesizers. Weber's music, far from being simply a bass recital, can turn into elaborate tone poems that in earlier times would have required the services of an orchestra.

CHAPTER SEVEN

BLUE AND GOLD

❛In one way or another, Armstrong fathered
all the trumpeters . . . Eldridge started
listening to him in 1931, at twenty, taking
cues from his dramatic storytelling intensity,
his logic, his gleaming high-note flourishes❜

GARY GIDDINS

The Trumpet

The most heinous crime to a classical wind player is
vibrato, the tremulous 'shaking' of a prolonged note
as opposed to hitting and sustaining it as close to the
sound of a tuning fork as possible. Wide vibrato at
the end notes became one of the most instantly
recognizable characteristics of the early jazz brass
style. So did devices like 'lip trills', and the muting of
the instrument's sound by capping the bell of the
horn. All kinds of handy props were pressed into

*British trombonist Paul Rutherford has acquired a
similar technique to German Albert Mangelsdorff,
but used it in more impressionistic free-music.*

service to act as mutes. The pre-recording-era
veteran, Buddy Bolden, used half a coconut shell, a
bathroom plunger and an old Derby hat. King
Oliver used a child's beach pail to try to capture those
earthy, folksy timbres. The early players also used
scales that frequently deployed the flattened 'blue'
notes on the thirds and sevenths.

Charles 'Buddy' Bolden is the earliest jazz brass
player of real significance, but since he was at large in
an era that preceded recording, none of his music has
passed into any other dimension but folklore. The
legend of Bolden runs that he owned both a
barbershop and a scandal-sheet in New Orleans, that
he lived fast to the point of self-destructiveness, and

died in a Louisiana mental institution in 1931, after nearly three decades of fitful insanity.

But the first jazz cornettist to record was Nick LaRocca of the Original Dixieland Jass Band, whose progress towards cutting the first-ever jazz recordings we have already touched on. LaRocca was the son of an Italian shoemaker who himself played cornet. As a teenager, he hung out with many of the bands of very young players who sporadically worked around New Orleans for pocket money. LaRocca was self-taught and couldn't read music, but he was a strong player and found work with 'Papa' Jack Laine, a local professional bandleader.

Listening to the sound of the O.D.J.B. today, few enough of what have since come to be regarded as jazz trademarks can be heard in it. Though syncopation of the notes are a cornerstone of the music, observation of the basic beat is scrupulous. LaRocca hints at toying with the pulse in some of his supportive playing but the bluesy intonation of 'bent notes' is missing.

If LaRocca was the first jazz-influenced cornettist to be heard on record, the first to emerge who clearly had absorbed the elements of jazz swing and intonation was Joseph 'King' Oliver. Not only a fine brass player, Oliver was a man with a disposition well suited to leadership, particularly of that volatile and mercurial entity that was a New Orleans jazz band.

By 1915, Oliver was regarded as one of the top flight jazz players in New Orleans. When the Original Dixieland Jass Band woke the world up to this new idiom, there was inevitably a domino effect, even on those playing a less commercially attractive version of it. The whirlwind took Oliver to Chicago, and Louis Armstrong with him. The recordings of their partnership in 1923 amounted to a revolution for jazz brass that has reverberated down the decades.

Oliver's own technique, though clearly inferior to Armstrong's, repeatedly demonstrates the unique resources of jazz as applied to the brass. His solos were

LEFT *Louis Armstrong, jazz music's first undisputed genius. As an unschooled teenager he could improvise harmony parts to other people's leads, and his improvisational flair enabled him to picture the entire long-term shape of a solo as he played it, and to toy audaciously with the placing of beats.*

RIGHT *Joe 'King' Oliver. His migration from New Orleans to Chicago led to the famous recordings that put the Southlands' contrapuntal ensemble sound on the map. Oliver was a strong, if limited, player but ingenious at variation on the most skeletal materials.*

leisurely and used limited melodic materials. His expression of those materials, however, was a revelation. 'Blue' notes were the underpinning of his style, but their exact pitching would be impossible to notate, because Oliver varied it continually. With a minimum of sounds, that would look mundane as a transcription, Oliver's feeling for the new-born jazz was so intimate that he could create a wealth of variation on them. He would add further variety by sliding from shrillness into reticence with the aid of the mute. And his accenting of the notes in relation to the underlying beat also defies any form of notation known to Western music.

The opportunity that King Oliver had provided for Louis Armstrong gave jazz its first genius – and maybe its greatest, because he had so little to go on. As has frequently been pointed out, there is no other way of accounting for the freedom and constantly regenerating embroidery with which the young

brassman would enhance the materials – and eventually lift them into another musical dimension entirely. The role of the cornet player in the New Orleans band up to that point required a tight and disciplined attention to ensemble duties, with only brief flirtations with solos in between.

Armstrong soon got a chance to show the world just what this new way of playing jazz trumpet would sound like. After his break from King Oliver, a short stint as the special effects man with Fletcher Henderson's orchestra, and some already scintillating session work with blues celebrities like Bessie Smith, Louis Armstrong went into the studios. It was 12 November 1925 and he had with him the band led by Lil Hardin that he had been appearing with at Chicago's Dreamland Cafe. That day was a landmark in jazz history.

The recordings of Louis Armstrong's Hot Fives and Hot Sevens represented the fiercest, warmest and

most inventive passages of jazz improvisation of the entire early phase of jazz – and over the three years that these studio bands cut the classic tracks, Armstrong was both refining his technique and increasingly turning to the trumpet instead of the cornet. It was a louder, brighter and altogether more imposing-sounding horn, and Armstrong was not put off by its apparent historical affiliation to classical and 'serious' music.

Armstrong's contribution to the sound of jazz was colossal. Listening to the fundamental 'hot' but cramped and rather deliberate playing of King Oliver makes the boldness of the younger man's style leap from the speakers. For a start, he could play the horn with a fullness and confidence in all registers – he wasn't simply strong in the middle, as most of his contemporaries were. His ability to pitch and hold high notes accurately virtually invented the use of an apparently 'freak' range of the horn for the jazz language. This was a skill he eventually turned into playing ensemble parts over sustained passages an octave above his partners.

LEFT *A contemporary of Louis Armstrong, Henry 'Red' Allen was nevertheless described as 'avant garde' in 1960 – not because he played in experimental idioms, but because his solo style was endlessly changing as jazz vocabulary expanded over the years.*

LEFT BELOW *Perfection of tone and a poetic lyrical imagination – Bix Beiderbecke rivalled Armstrong as an improvisor, but his rhythmic sense was more predictable and his playing partners less creative. Some of his performances however, notably 'I'm Coming Virginia' and 'Singin' the Blues', are deservedly regarded as classics.*

the shape of his inventions over a longer time-span. Consequently he was able to construct music as substantial and lasting as the work of concert music's great melodists – and furthermore, to conceive it, as much European music originally was, on the hoof. He was also ingenious at varying the timing of notes in relation to the basic pulse. Even in his secondary role to Oliver's cornet, it's possible to hear Armstrong hitting parts of a phrase behind the beat, then playing close to it for the remainder of the phrase. By the late Twenties he had become so confident about this that very few of the total of notes in a chorus actually hit the beat at all.

Armstrong's immediate contemporary – born in the same year – was Tommy Ladnier. But Ladnier's conception was much closer to Oliver's than Armstrong's, though he was a good blues player. The comet of Armstrong's progress across the firmament of jazz was a hard act to follow, but some brass players quickly began to come close to it. One of the best was Hot Lips Page, another excellent blues player who worked around Kansas City in the Thirties and whose sound was at times mistaken for Armstrong's. Another was Cladys 'Jabbo' Smith, a musician launched by the Brunswick record company as a rival to Armstrong. And he very nearly was: a player of startling fire and imagination. Max Kaminsky and Wild Bill Davison were also white musicians of the Chicago school who took their inspiration from Armstrong.

Muggsy Spanier, Red Nichols and Phil Napoleon were the 1920s' white equivalents in New York; New York jazz was distanced from the inspirational proximity of the best black players. The finest white trumpeter of the period was undoubtedly Leon 'Bix' Beiderbecke, who had begun his short but passionate affair with jazz by learning Nick LaRocca's cornet solos from the Original Dixieland band note for note.

Beiderbecke's life was short, and ruined by alcohol, but his talents were undimmed until his health was finally broken. He had a stunningly perfect tone, and his melodic inventiveness was probably superior to Armstrong's. His use of dissonant notes to delay the progress of an improvisation to a consonant or resolved point was daring even by the standards of modern jazz, and he eschewed 'blue' notes in favour of whole-tone intervals. He did not, however, possess Armstrong's looseness in rhythm, or approach the black trumpeter's astonishing willingness to abandon most of the usual semaphoring of where the beat was. His sense of the shape of the solo, however, was often dazzling – as it is on 'Singin' the Blues', with a pattern of statement, reappraisal and then final summary of all that has been asserted in the first four bars.

Bunny Berigan was Beiderbecke's natural succes-

Though he was as well equipped with the blues and folk instrumental dialects of slurs and elided notes as any other player of the time, he used them sparingly for variation and not as a means of connecting the passage together. In all, Armstrong's voice on trumpet arrived like a hurricane in the jazz world.

But it is Armstrong's sense of shape and purpose in a solo that makes sense of all this dazzling technique. Frequently he will include a 'landmark' of a figure with a particular recognizable cadence in each of several choruses, though each version of the phrase will be subtly varied in such a way as to suggest a climactic or descendent momentum when the whole sequence is played together.

Throughout the course of jazz, from New Orleans to free music, the most frequently encountered weakness in solos is incoherence – the playing of fragments of melody, or arpeggios that fit a particular chord but seem cut off by an invisible fence from the ideas that follow. Armstrong seemed able, like the most gifted figures in all types of music, to foresee

sor, and another of jazz music's short-lived figures, but it was Bobby Hackett who adapted the style and sustained it well into the modern period. Rex Stewart did the same with the Fletcher Henderson big band of the early Thirties, and later with Duke Ellington. Stewart used the mute and the half-valve effect with more consistency than most, and could unleash a bone-shaking growl into the bargain.

The Duke Ellington Orchestra supplied many excellent trumpeters – like Bubber Miley, Cootie Williams, Ray Nance and, later, Clark Terry – partly because the band's early years saw a strong emphasis on the 'jungle-sound'. A Beiderbecke-like purity of intonation has little place in this style.

If clarity and an almost architectural deliberation in setting blocks of phrasing against each other were characteristics of both Armstrong and Beiderbecke, albeit in different ways, a more legato style that would make the phrasing flow was being developed by a different breed of player. Henry 'Red' Allen was one of the first – a highly melodic player, who nevertheless shaped his solos with unpredictable contours, calm and stately passages alternating with nervous, stuttery phrases, with the blues clearly at the heart of it. In 1960, the modern composer Don Ellis described Allen as continuing to deserve the title 'avant-garde'. Allen replaced King Oliver in the Luis Russell band in 1929, and his style was developed by musicians like Roy Eldridge, Buck Clayton, Harry Edison and Charlie Shavers. Allen himself went through something of a renaissance in the 1950s when he modified his style to a more reflective modernism suggestive of Miles Davis.

Eldridge and Shavers were bold and technically powerful players; Clayton and Edison had a more discreet and gentle style but their melodic inventiveness was ahead of their period and earned them star status with the Count Basie Orchestra of the 1930s. Clayton avoided bold effects and the wild, splashy style of many of the trumpeters of the period, preferring a kind of gentle, ruminative lyricism, full of deft, understated phrases and delicate vibrato – emotionalism of a distinctly off-the-sleeve kind. Edison later had a successful career in the recording studios, and with celebrated singers such as Billie Holiday and Frank Sinatra. His way of embellishing a song consistently enhanced it without drawing excessive attention to himself.

RIGHT *'Sound-effects' trumpeters, who could hit stratospheric high notes, were not just features of the big-band era. Cuban Arturo Sandoval not only has a piccolo-like range, he also uses his exceptional technique to play jazz, salsa, and variations on European straight music.*

RIGHT *Ruby Braff, a trumpeter young enough to have been a bebopper, but who opted for preserving the earlier Chicago styles. A fine interpreter of standards, and a musician of grace and taste.*

LEFT *John Birks 'Dizzy' Gillespie. His restless experimenting with the harmonies of swing tunes led him down much the same path as Charlie Parker. Together, they were the two most famous names of bebop.*

Some trumpeters belonged to the generation that developed modern jazz, but continued to play in earlier styles themselves. One of the most fascinating is Ruby Braff, a man of Miles Davis's generation who nevertheless has made a perfectionist pursuit of the trumpet methods of the swing era and earlier. He is recognized as an invaluable nurturer of those traditions now that most of the originals have departed, his style a blend of Armstrong's, Berigan's and Wild Bill Davison's.

There have also been those whose role has been primarily as 'special effects' players – like Cat Anderson in the Ellington band, who could play stratospheric high notes. One who used this technique within a context of his own is Maynard Ferguson, who emerged from the Stan Kenton Orchestra as one of the most technically startling of all performers on his instrument. Cuban Arturo Sandoval has much the same technical command, but hitches it to salsa and Cuban rhythms, as well as Latin adaptations of European classical music with the group Irakere.

The cornerstone of modern trumpet is John Birks 'Dizzy' Gillespie, and the bridge from Armstrong to him is Roy Eldridge. Eldridge's playing is capable of imperious swings from a stratospheric register to the sonorous depths of the instrument in a manner quite distinct from Armstrong. He can also produce a sustained operatic intensity rare in jazz, so frequently a music of hurried or abandoned effects.

Gillespie came from the South, the son of a bricklayer who was also an amateur musician. His father recognized his talent and got him a musical education. This gave the young Gillespie a head-start in theory that was to profoundly influence the development of bebop. Though he modelled himself on Roy Eldridge, he quickly came to believe that he would never adequately capture the older man's unique sound, and looked for ways of his own to develop.

With the Teddy Hill band, though he often put his job on the line by the horseplay that earned him his nickname, Gillespie established himself as a very superior kind of swing trumpeter. He had a first-class technique, a good sound and a growing audacity of solo construction. In 1939, Gillespie joined Cab Calloway – and this time the trumpeter's unruly behaviour, compounded by the bandleader's dislike of the unusual harmonies he was beginning to explore, did earn him the sack. So he began sitting in with the band that drummer Kenny Clarke had put together at Minton's.

Like Parker, Gillespie began to draw raw material for improvising not just from the notes related to the chord of the tune he was playing, but also from briefly sliding into another chord a semitone away from the fundamental one. He would play a short

Miles Davis, who began performing with Charlie Parker's group when barely out of his teens, was startling proof that fast technique isn't everything. Davis' playing was often shaky but his swing, timbre and power to edit his solos mercilessly made him a unique jazz voice.

passage of the components of a major chord over a tune in a minor key. He would also substitute for the standard chords of a song a sequence of different ones that were nonetheless harmonically related. But, as with Armstrong, an even more important step forward was in rhythm.

Gillespie's playing changed after 1946, when he founded his epochal bebop big band. He became more interested in Latin (particularly Cuban) rhythms, and his playing lost its occasionally stuttery quality and became effortlessly virtuosic at apparently any tempo and in any harmonic pattern. Even into his seventies, Gillespie has almost miraculously retained much of his fire and technique, and his big band has recently resurfaced, to devastating effect.

Several remarkable trumpeters emerged from under Gillespie's coat-tails, either directly or at one remove, and became the dominant figures of the first and second waves of bebop. Among them were Howard McGhee, Fats Navarro, Red Rodney, Kenny Dorham, Clifford Brown, Lee Morgan and Miles Davis.

Navarro died young, but had quickly become an architect of hard bop, regarded by some as the idiom's most perfect trumpeter. Brown, Dorham and Lee Morgan were all in Navarro's mould. His harmonic awareness was subtle; the order and deliberation of his solos gave them a classical poise. Miles Davis had worked with Charlie Parker in the late 1940s; he had started under the Gillespie influence, but quickly emerged from it to become the third crucial trumpet voice in jazz after Armstrong and Gillespie.

Davis was temperamentally and musically of quite a different mould to the older trumpet stars. His playing was often subdued and technically unremarkable, rarely venturing into the high register. After the first bebop excursions, he began to eschew the bop habit of packing hailstones of miniscule subdivisions of notes into the structure of the tune. Davis's playing was more selective and more contemplative, but it nevertheless swung as irresistably as the music of any of the previous pioneers of jazz.

After he left Parker in 1949, Davis became leader on a session involving a number of white musicians (arranger Gil Evans, saxophonists Gerry Mulligan and Lee Konitz). These produced a soft, plush,

TOP LEFT *Chet Baker, the white Miles Davis, though less affecting in his use of texture.*

TOP *Jon Faddis, often a soloist in the Dizzy Gillespie Orchestra, is treated as a musical son by the older man. Faddis' tone is clean, and he is unfazed by the most breakneck tempo.*

ABOVE *Wynton Marsalis, one of the most popular of trumpeters. Marsalis, who performs as a soloist with symphony orchestras as well, has made a point of refurbishing jazz history and much of his work draws on the lessons of 1950s and 1960s Miles Davis.*

restrained kind of orchestral jazz eventually dubbed the 'Birth of the Cool' sessions. Davis's own soloing was distinctive but unsteady. It appeared to be as much influenced by the Beiderbecke school at several removes as it was by Gillespie. But it had absorbed the harmonic and rhythmic advances of bop at the same time as rejecting one of that idiom's central features – loquacity (and sometimes downright verbosity). Miles Davis's playing became a byword for understatement. His sound was soft, he frequently used a mute to create an even more squeezed, reluctant tone, he would stay within a single octave for long passages, and his phrasing was fragmentary rather than legato, or continuous.

Davis dropped out of music with a heroin problem in the early Fifties, but defeated it and came back, making a devastating appearance at the 1955 Newport Jazz Festival. He appeared with a band that had both energy and drive (Philly Joe Jones, John Coltrane) and the sharp contrast of Davis's own highly edited, restrained playing. It was increasingly clear that the trumpeter's more modest art lay in his use of unexpected placings of notes and equally unexpected pauses and delays. He would also frequently form a note that very explicitly curved away from its original pitch, or hold a single note for longer periods than Gillespie or Navarro ever would.

Davis continually revised his work. He reacted against the sardonic, elbowing, competitive small group style of hard bop by creating tone-poems with Gil Evans where his trumpet was often the only soloing instrument against an orchestra. He also reacted against it by taking scales rather than chords as the basis for improvising (initially with 'Milestones' but most famously with 'Kind of Blue'). He developed a tighter, less incantatory version of Coltrane's mid-Sixties work in a band with a Coltrane-ish saxophonist (Wayne Shorter, who had come from Art Blakey's group) and an Elvin Jones-influenced drummer (Tony Williams) and then turned to amalgamations of jazz and rock in the late Sixties.

Davis's trumpet sound during this period became at times untypically fierce and squalling (often aided by electronic bugs). It has only recently returned to its romantic, balladeering early character on a number of covers of pop tunes that the trumpeter has recorded since his comeback from illness in the Eighties.

Other trumpeters who adopted the soft approach included Chet Baker and Art Farmer. Baker, a white musician, is the closest to the Fifties Davis style. He became a star in a band co-led by Gerry Mulligan, and his technique progressively developed through the Sixties, though long layoffs from music prevented Baker from achieving all that he might have done. He died in an accident in 1988.

Clifford Brown, who died in a road crash in 1956, was another brass player whose contribution was stunted. He was a disciple of Fats Navarro who quickly developed his own blend of Gillespie-like heat and longer melodic lines of cool jazz. Brown had made an impression with the Lionel Hampton band of 1953, and then with Max Roach in a memorable small group for the next three years. His method of structuring a solo, particularly in its even, pulsating ebb and flow of accents, recalled Navarro, but he had a punch and vigour that his mentor's slightly studious calmness lacked. Some have compared the torrential stream of Brown's ideas, the headlong urgency of their momentum, to Charlie Parker's own.

Brown spawned a legion of trumpeters who were in the forefront of hard bop, the idiom that tried to ignore the then fashionable cool school in all ways except the approach to structuring improvisation. These musicians included Donald Byrd, Lee Morgan, Bill Hardman, Nat Adderley, Woody Shaw, Booker Little and Freddie Hubbard. A younger generation of players including Jon Faddis, Hannibal Marvin Peterson, Terumasa Hino and Wynton Marsalis have followed the same lead.

But the prevailing mood of many of the 'free' players of the 1960s was to try to take jazz back to some of its more random, unpremeditated and folk-influenced roots. This was also the direction pursued by the greatest and most influential of free-jazz trumpeters – Don Cherry. Cherry came to the fore as an erratic and sometimes frantic-sounding cohort of Ornette Coleman's, though he had formerly been a promising bop trumpeter. But Cherry's new sound quickly became unique. He elected to use a 'pocket trumpet', like a shrunken cornet, which gave his music a distinctive, blustery quality. His tone often sounds as if he is doleful, but the construction of his phrases is quite the opposite. He frequently uses short figures, and his rhythmic sense is acute. Many of his improvised figures are lilting and tuneful enough to be sung, though he will often contrast them with bubbling, fast, unaccented flares of sound. And following Cherry's move to Europe, his music began to absorb elements from Bali, Tibet, India, the Middle East and China.

Subsequent free-jazz trumpeters like Lester Bowie, Leo Smith, Butch Morris, Mike Mantler and Don Ellis have all taken a lead from Cherry. Ellis, who had also studied composer George Russell's distinctive scalar principles, began playing a special quarter-toned trumpet in the 1960s, to explore further some of the subdivisions of tones that Cherry

LEFT *Canadian-born trumpeter Ken Wheeler emigrated to Britain in the 1950s, working early on with the John Dankworth band, and then virtually all European modernists of stature. His sound is pensive, but scattered with unexpected animation, often expressed in wide interval leaps.*

RIGHT *Kid Ory, most famous of the early 'tailgate' trombonists. Ory's big, effusive tone and slurred sounds washed around the busier activities of the New Orleans front line musicians.*

was using on a relatively orthodox instrument.

Bowie, who works with the Art Ensemble of Chicago, is both a contemporary player and a fervent defender of the vocalized styles of the early trumpeters and frequently uses these devices from early 'hot' playing in his solos.

In Europe, trumpeters have included Kenny Wheeler, Harry Beckett, Ian Carr, Enrico Rava, Tomasz Stanko, Palle Mikkelborg and Manfred Schoof. Wheeler is a Canadian living in Britain, a thoughtful performer clearly influenced by Miles Davis but with a clean, gunmetal tone and a distinctive manner of phrasing involving wide interval jumps. Carr is also a Miles Davis admirer, and has similarly deployed that trumpet style in jazz–rock fusion bands. Beckett, one of the most modest but immediately recognizable of European trumpeters, originally hails from the West Indies. His amiable-sounding improvisations frequently resemble a long, unrestrained chuckle.

The Trombone

The first role for the trombone in New Orleans and early jazz was as a kind of connective tissue for the multiplicity of instrumental voices in the band, and also as a complement to – or even a substitute for – the

tuba or the bass. In other words, its function was rhythmic and harmonic. The 'tailgate' style of playing the instrument – long smearing glissandos that seemed to function like someone hauling or pushing the phrases of the melody instruments into each other – had its most celebrated practitioner in Kid Ory. The method got its name from the trombonist's position on the band-wagons that roamed around New Orleans advertising the Monday night dances – sitting on the back facing the road, so that the slide didn't hit the other members of the ensemble.

The early trombonists, like Ory, Charlie Green, and the O.D.J.B.'s George Brunies, didn't regard themselves as soloists, even in the sense that they extemporized solo-like counter-melodies behind their colleagues. The available styles didn't depart much from a slurring New Orleans technique, a brisk white one, and a higher, smoother one that was virtually Jimmy Harrison's invention. This method he combined with an atmosphere of considerable intensity and emotion and a throwback to New Orleans with a broad vibrato sound. Harrison, a performer with the Fletcher Henderson Orchestra, gave the trombone respect as a solo voice, and did it with an incisiveness of attack and a precision of

intonation that came close to the sound of the more orthodox solo horns.

Miff Mole, a white performer, was close to Harrison's talent – and he in turn helped found the reputations of two trombone players whose names eventually figured much more substantially in the jazz history books. These were Tommy Dorsey, better known as a swing bandleader, and Weldon Leo 'Jack' Teagarden.

Teagarden was also a good technician, strongly influenced by Harrison (with whom he sometimes played), but he was an all-round musician of greater expressiveness and idiosyncrasy. He became a regular partner of Louis Armstrong – both as an instrumentalist and as a singer – and his feeling for the blues was intelligent and sensitive. Teagarden had a gentle yet

flexible approach to trombone improvising (Bix Beiderbecke, with some impatience, accused him of playing flute on trombone), and a measured, drawling manner suggestive of his native Texas.

His arrival on the scene was a substantial boost to the confidence of those attempting to forge a new language for the instrument. Where Harrison was heated, Teagarden was charmingly offhand. His phrasing rarely followed a routine and he constantly varied the beat, like Armstrong. He got rid of the vibrato in the 1930s, and was assumed to be a valve trombonist by many listeners. Even by the point at which the 'cool school' emerged, Teagarden's playing was regarded as a model to trombonists. Duke Ellington's trombonists – like the trumpeters – were celebrated for the special effects they could deliver, and Joseph 'Tricky Sam' Nanton made a name for himself as an expert in the technique of 'growl' trombone.

Many other fine trombonists emerged during the swing era: J.C. Higginbotham brought a fierce, percussive and earthy sound to the instrument, habitually leaping big intervals; Vic Dickenson produced a wry and deceptively simple lyricism; Trummy Young (who worked with Jimmy Lunceford) had a bristling, pyrotechnical, bravura style; and Bill Harris played with a speed and clarity that genuinely rivalled the sprightlier horns.

Dickenson in fact minimizes the melodic improvisation he applies to a tune, preferring a faintly mocking brand of gentle embroidery full of groaning sounds, sardonic snorts and exclamations, all of it rolling purposefully along on a graceful built-in swing.

Bill Harris's recording of 'Bijou' with the Woody Herman band in 1944 made the jazz world realize what a force he had become as well, a mixture of busy phrasing and baying-at-the-moon wistfulness that anticipated modernists like Roswell Rudd. For a long time this was the passage that all aspiring trombonists turned to for enlightenment.

But the first true bebop trombonist of stature was Indianapolis-born J.J. Johnson. He has been compared with Dizzy Gillespie for his impact on the instrument. He freed its fast technique to cope with bebop tempos, but didn't lose the brilliant gleam of the trumpet-like tone in the process. Johnson had begun as a swing musician, and like all swing trombonists, he possessed a smooth, legato technique highly unsuited to the eighth-note barrages of bop. But when he abandoned the traditional method of playing the instrument, he abandoned it conclusively. His immense technique helped him to banish slurred notes, the standard vibrato or indeterminate pitches. Though his sound wasn't insistent or declamatory, it was more decisive in its accuracy and purity than any previous trombonist in jazz. Danish

OPPOSITE TOP LEFT
Jack Teagarden, an idiosyncratic vocalist as well as a light-toned, attractively offhand trombonist. He was a frequent and popular partner of Louis Armstrong's.

ABOVE *Vic Dickenson was one of the most humorous and eccentric of trombonists, often preferring snorts, groans and interrogative sounds to more studious variations on the melody.*

LEFT *J.J. Johnson, a founding figure of bebop trombone – an idiom at first thought to be beyond the scope of the instrument. Fast and trumpet-like, Johnson was the diametric opposite of Vic Dickenson.*

trombonist Kai Winding was of Johnson's school, a Benny Goodman sideman who later joined Stan Kenton.

The 'bebop school' has spawned a large number of young trombonists who now take the technical demands in their stride, and most of whom have ended up working in the idiom of hard bop. They have included Curtis Fuller, Jimmy Knepper (a Charles Mingus sideman), Julian Priester (who has worked with Max Roach and Herbie Hancock), Slide Hampton, Jimmy Cleveland and Bob Brookmeyer.

Knepper, a brilliant technician, nevertheless harks back to the pre-Johnson era of soaring, seamless phrasing, and his links with Bill Harris are clear.

Brookmeyer, a frequent partner of saxophonist Jimmy Guiffre in the Fifties and Sixties, came up under the influence of Wells, Dickenson and Harris. He plays the valve trombone, which has a little more built-in flexibility. Through it he affects the excitable, impulsive, coarser methods of earlier players, the accuracy and speed of the modernists, some of Dickenson's humour, and a thumping of the beat very close to the pulse. He is sometimes prone to over-embroidery, as if he were desperate to pass himself off as a saxophonist.

Frank Rosolino, a Kenton musician, also descended from the Johnson school. Urbie Green and Al Grey are unclassifiable performers who can work in virtually any style, Grey if anything being a student of Tricky Sam Nanton.

Out of the free jazz of the 1960s, two key trombonists emerged. Grachan Moncur III and Roswell Rudd. Rudd was an ex-Dixieland player who came to prominence with New York's Jazz Composers' Orchestra Association. His earthy sound and feeling for blues was readily transplanted into the free explorations of the period, when a more direct sound without the complexities of bebop was being sought. An admirer of Bill Harris (he has even dedicated records to the Herman sideman), Rudd has been devoted to the task of restoring the expressiveness to the instrument that the technical demands of bebop excluded. He can be boppish, dissonant or primitive as the circumstances take him.

And in Europe, a number of practitioners on the instrument began to reveal their own special contributions. The most remarkable has been the German Albert Mangelsdorff, who has been one of the foremost trombone players in the world since the 1950s. Mangelsdorff has developed a technique that enables him to blow one note and sing a different one, and then to obtain even more levels of harmony through the overtones created by the collision of the two sounds.

Paul Rutherford, an English musician who also began with Dixieland, has similarly explored the potential of overtones and combined playing and

speech, taking it into more remote areas of free improvisation than Mangelsdorff.

Other notable Europeans include Gunther Christmann, Willem van Manen, Connie Bauer, and Englishwoman Annie Whitehead – apprenticed with the all-woman danceband led by veteran, Ivy Benson, but now developing a personal style that links pop, African jazz, and electronics.

Three Americans have come to the fore on the instrument in recent years. In the more orthodox field there has been Bill Watrous, a remarkable technician with a huge, penetrating sound who has done as much as anyone to expand the instrument's range from the original three octaves to something like five and a half. George Lewis is capable of functioning in both tonal orchestral settings (frequently Gil Evans's bands) and on the European free scene, where he will sometimes work with musicians whose explicit interest in the jazz tradition has become difficult to discern. In this context Lewis often augments the sound of his horn with electronics, and sometimes plays 'unaccompanied' with a synthesizer that will actually duet contrasting lines with him. Steve Turre, who plays with Dizzy Gillespie, is a big, booming player with a surprisingly delicate melodic imagination. And Ray Anderson, a free player who has latterly performed a blend of funk, blues and abstract music, is similarly possessed of great virtuosity and at times some of the explosiveness of Higginbotham.

CHAPTER EIGHT

LIQUID MUSIC

> ' He'd take an E flat clarinet and play in the orchestra. He didn't know what key we were playing in, but you couldn't lose him. That's the truth. Never saw anything like it '

PETER BOCAGE OF SIDNEY BECHET

Entwining the lines of the trumpet and trombone 'like ivy' was the way Joachim Berendt described the role of the clarinet in the New Orleans ensemble. The great trio of early clarinet players is Johnny Dodds, Jimmy Noone, and Sidney Bechet.

Dodds joined the King Oliver Band in 1920. His sound on their early recordings is direct and soulful, and his tone is abrasive and jostling with growls and scrapings. In contrast to Noone's, Dodds's technique was more uncertain in fast passages, and inclined to

As much at home with a Mozart concerto as with jazz, Benny Goodman was one of the swing era's consummate technicians.

squeakiness. But he was a fine blues player, like many of the early jazz musicians.

Jimmie Noone came from Cut Off, Louisiana, and was originally a guitarist. Bechet taught him to play the clarinet, and from 1917 through the Twenties he shuttled back and forth between New Orleans and Chicago. Noone was a better technician than most at the time, and he had a warm, inviting sound, which made him a regular soloist with bands led by King Oliver, Louis Armstrong and others. A famous, but possibly apocryphal story about Noone goes that one of his solos was once transcribed by Maurice Ravel, who was then told by the first clarinet in a symphony orchestra that playing such a thing was impossible.

Following on the heels of these men came Albert Nicholas, also Armstrong's age, and New Orleans-born. By 1923 he was fronting his own band in his hometown, in between gigs for King Oliver. What characterized Nicholas's sound was a warm tone, but an approach more graceful and less wayward than Bechet's, fluid and less scattered with rasps and growls. Like many of the New Orleans players he had a relaxed feel for ensemble work and for improvising a harmony against other musicians' lines.

Along with Nicholas came Omer Simeon and Barney Bigard. Simeon played with Jelly Roll Morton and was the bandleader's favourite clarinet-tist, similar to Noone, and his tone was good. Bigard, from New Orleans (born 1906) and favouring the looping, relaxed Creole style, was notable for his work with Duke Ellington in the Thirties, and with Armstrong in the Fifties.

With Bigard came a transition on the instrument from New Orleans music to swing. In the white circles in Chicago, a number of other clarinettists were travelling the same road – like Frank Teschemacher, Jimmy Dorsey, and Pee Wee Russell. All had their own characteristic sounds. Tesche-macher used a great deal of smear and palette-knife glissando effects, Dorsey was bold and assured, and Russell was perhaps the most idiosyncratic. He was fond of hovering in the lower register. His sound would fluctuate between being soft to the point of evaporation and shrill and clawing at the outer edge of pitch before spiralling back on to the unbearably delayed resolution. He would also deliver a tapestry of jaunty trills, manipulations of the beat and an anxious, almost manic tone at quicker tempos.

The most celebrated clarinettist of the swing era was Benny Goodman. A classically trained per-former who also occasionally performed as a classical soloist, Goodman's technique was complete and his approach to jazz open, amiable and communicative. He could make an impact at the lowest volume. His solos were balanced, poised and used dynamics more effectively than almost any other clarinettist. And his phrasing had an alert, silvery impulsiveness about it that belied the immense weight of the musical knowledge that backed it up. Goodman was as much at home with a Mozart clarinet concerto as he was with jazz, and he commissioned classical composers like Bela Bartok and Aaron Copland to write clarinet pieces for him. Buddy De Franco in the 1950s was the first clarinettist to seriously threaten Goodman's pre-eminence as a technician.

The swing era also produced Artie Shaw and Woody Herman, who led big bands of their own, Jimmy Hamilton (a discreet, soft-toned performer who worked with Ellington), Buster Bailey and

BELOW *One of the first great New Orleans clarinettists, Johnny Dodds.*

RIGHT *Some of the warmest and most supple New Orleans clarinet solos came from the horn of Albert Nicholas.*

BOTTOM *Charles Ellsworth 'Pee Wee' Russell, the possessor of one of the most unique sounds of all jazz clarinettists – a blend of shrewd dynamics and skewed, exclamatory intonation.*

BOTTOM RIGHT *Clarinettist Edmond Hall's technique was equal to Goodman's, but his sound exhibited an almost threatening grittiness.*

Edmond Hall. Hall was comparable to Goodman in his impact on swing clarinet playing. He worked extensively with Eddie Condon and was as sharp, tough and urgent sounding as Goodman was urbane, liquid and relaxed. Hall's vibrato whirred like a motor, he constantly seemed to be in a hurry, and his intonation was pulsing with colour and vocalized effects.

A prominent modernist on the instrument, who developed a form of jazz that was a tributary of bop rather than in its main course, is Jimmy Guiffre. Like Pee Wee Russell, Guiffre was initially fond of the lower register – and like the 'cool school' musicians, he was looking for equivalents to the style of Lester Young. Young himself had even recorded on clarinet a few times, enough to suggest that his impact on the instrument could have been substantial.

The German Rolf Kuhn and the American Tony Scott have also made significant impressions. Kuhn has a Goodmanesque soundness of technique, on to which he has added contemporary sounds from the avant-garde and from jazz-rock. Scott, a powerful performer with a huge sound, has spent little time in the States since the use of the clarinet appeared to be dwindling, and has acted as an ambassador and teacher for both the instrument and for jazz in general all over the world.

A performer more generally renowned as a flautist and alto saxophonist introduced a new instrument to

the jazz line-up in the 1960s. Eric Dolphy was another highly creative jazz musician whose productive life was short, but he brought the bass clarinet into jazz, creating a style of dark, wriggling low tones, slashing, banshee-like runs and an emphatic intonation of single notes that sound like drumbeats.

Dolphy's ideas have been followed up by Europeans Willem Breuker, John Surman, Michel Portal and Gunter Hampel. Multi-instrumentalist Anthony Braxton, a towering figure on the free scene on most reed instruments, has modified the use of the clarinet in jazz in ways that are appropriate to the transformations in melody that have swept the avant-garde.

CHAPTER NINE

HORNS OF PLENTY

6 The saxophone is really the first
modern instrument 9

ARCHIE SHEPP

The saxophone, which was invented by a Belgian, Adolphe Sax, in the middle of the last century, ostensibly in an effort to improve the tone of the bass clarinet, has been booed on-stage in most forms of music, martial music excepted. It has generally been played with softness and restraint, or even downright sentimentality, in both classical orchestras and dance bands – what one critic called its 'sherbet-like tone'. It was a long time before anybody played it in such a manner as to achieve the aggressive, penetrative

Tenorist, actor, bon viveur – Dexter Gordon is one of the jazz personalities who warrants the label of 'larger than life', in every possible respect.

impact of a trumpet. Since the saxophone is capable of being played with the agility of a clarinet, which it closely resembles in construction, the potential of the machine for jazz use was dormant for a surprisingly long time.

Sax had sold many of his original instruments to the French army, and the horn's use in military bands spread rapidly from the late 19th century. But though the instrument might well have been fairly plentiful in the bazaars of secondhand instruments in New Orleans around 1900, it was the clarinet – which already had a firm place in the Creole musical education – that was the natural reed instrument for early jazz players.

One of the first influential jazz saxophonists was not primarily a clarinettist however. Adrian Rollini, a classically trained white New Yorker who was skilled on both piano and xylophone, began playing saxophone in 1920. His tone was good, and his phrasing surprisingly agile considering that his chosen instrument was an anachronism in jazz – the bass saxophone. Rollini performed with many of the best white musicians – including Bix Beiderbecke and violinist Joe Venuti – and his resonant, powerful sound became an early model for Coleman Hawkins. But the real impact on saxophone improvising did come from a clarinettist – Sidney Bechet.

Bechet established the saxophone as a natural voice in jazz, and did it with much the same panache as Louis Armstrong was doing with the trumpet. Duke Ellington said of Bechet: 'I think he was the most unique man ever to be in this music.' His impact may not, in the end, have been quite so critical to the advancement of jazz as Armstrong's was, but there's little enough to choose between them. In technical audacity, in an instinct for perceiving a different way of using an old form, and in an overwhelming confidence that the new way is the right one, the two were distinctly alike. Bechet learned the clarinet so fast that by the age of 11 or 12 he was already working regularly in New Orleans, with both juvenile and adult bands.

But Bechet was more of a wanderer than Armstrong, and his wanderings changed the course of jazz. It was in London in 1920, on a tour with a kind of early pops orchestra, the Southern Syncopated Orchestra, that he came across a soprano saxophone, an instrument he had already become interested in, in the window of J.F. Lafleur's music shop at 147 Wardour Street. He practised on it in the shop for some time, and insisted that a double-octave key be added to it before he laid out the 30 guineas for its purchase. Within days, Bechet was playing fluently on the instrument, and felt that its increased carrying power broadened his scope as a musician – though some of his colleagues in the Southern Syncopated Orchestra were not so sure.

By the end of the Twenties Bechet had freed himself from ragtime's stiffness. Almost as if he were circularly breathing, the tone is both substantial and penetrative. It is coloured with all manner of distortions and growls, most particularly by the musician's vibrato, which is wide, intense and adds spectacularly to the sense of expectancy and climax.

In 1932, Bechet's recording of 'I Found a New Baby', with trumpeter Tommy Ladnier, demonstrated the saxophonist's continuing ability to flatten every performer in the same studio as him. Ladnier in fact – normally a selective and reserved musician – seems stung by Bechet's unquenchable mastery to a series of unexpectedly anguished wails and shouts on

the horn. 'Maple Leaf Rag', however, with the same band, reveals Bechet at full pressure, an unceasing flow of ideas played with blistering power; as does 'Shag' – one of the first, if not the first themeless jazz recording, improvised on the 'I Got Rhythm' sequence and notable for some fervent, yearning, long note sounds from the soprano.

Bechet retired from jazz for a while in the 1930s, and ran a gents' outfitters with Ladnier. But with the

Sidney Bechet, here playing the soprano, established the saxophone as a natural voice in jazz, with as substantial an impact on the instrument as Armstrong had on the trumpet

revival of interest in New Orleans music, and a hit recording of 'Summertime' for the new Blue Note label, Bechet came back. He even jammed with Charlie Parker at the 1949 Nice Jazz Festival and lived in Paris throughout the Fifties until his death in 1959.

Bechet's most enthusiastic admirer, and one of the next authoritative voices to emerge on the saxophone, was Duke Ellington sideman Johnny Hodges.

Hodges, along with two other prominent altoists – Benny Carter and Willie Smith – made a powerful impression in the early Thirties.

For a long time, Hodges's sound was virtually synonymous with the image of the saxophone in jazz. His tone was warm, his vibrato resonant and impassioned, and his tendency to slide notes into each other gave his music a sensuous and seductive charm. Hodges had worked with Bechet around Boston in

the early Twenties, occasionally deputizing for him, and assiduously copying his ideas on to the alto saxophone.

But it was with Duke Ellington that Hodges's sound became most closely associated, and it was Ellington's music to which he lent his most sensitive and lustrous interpretations. On slow tunes he was devastating. But he could also swing effortlessly – at either end of the tempo range. The influence of Bechet would be extensively audible in his use of pitch changes and blue notes, and he would frequently construct solos with constant dynamic changes, as if the music were swelling and fading like an erratic radio signal. Like Bechet too, Hodges had learned early on how to vary the beats on which his accents fell. The result was that his rhythmic variation played a large part in the inexorable sense of momentum in his solos, even in ballads.

Hodges joined the Ellington band in 1928, and was making an impact from early on. Coleman Hawkins was also making an impression, but on the tenor saxophone, with the influential Fletcher Henderson

band. These two men, along with Bechet and a Chicago player, Bud Freeman, were the most creative saxophonists of the early Thirties.

But Hawkins had the head-start of technical knowledge. He had begun to learn the piano as a child, then the cello, and had taken up the saxophone when he was nine. He was born in Missouri but went to school in Chicago, which gave him a chance to hear the transplanted New Orleans players, notably clarinettist Jimmy Noone.

As a college student, Hawkins investigated harmonic theory – unusual for the jazz players of the day. And by the time he was invited to join Mamie Smith's Jazz Hounds in 1922, he already had a great deal more harmonic knowledge than most of his fellow saxophonists.

In the first phase, Hawkins's sound was abrasive and his phrasing clipped. Through the Thirties he became smoother, more elegant. He was fascinated by bop, having sufficient harmonic awareness to understand what the music was founded on, though its offbeat phrasing threw him. And from the bebop

era onward, he became more fragmented and angular. But throughout he was the consummate improviser. Until his decline in his last years, he almost invariably enhanced the fabric of every tune he played, and his ability to improve on his raw materials was one of the most spectacular instances of this particular facility in all of jazz.

Hawkins's seven-league stride in jazz was his conviction that the harmony of a tune provided more potential as a basis for improvisation than its melody. Most of Louis Armstrong's quoted comments on his methods mention the pre-eminence of the melody, constantly echoing in the back of his head as he played. As a self-taught player, it was almost inevitable that Armstrong would treat this as seriously, but so did the idiom he operated in.

The pioneer of manipulating the basic harmonies of tunes was the pianistic genius Art Tatum. Some of the Fletcher Henderson sidemen heard Tatum in a club in the late Twenties and were dumbfounded by his cavalier treatment of the foundations of the music that had seemed sacrosanct. Hawkins is quoted as being particularly impressed, possibly because his musical training revealed more to him of what Tatum was actually doing. It became the basis of the saxophonist's method, and of that of many saxophonists to follow.

Hawkins became fascinated by the *arpeggios* of chords – how a melody line would sound constructed from the component notes of the chords of a tune played separately, but in any order, rather than as a set of variations on the original theme. This had come naturally to piano players for some time, who were used to thinking harmonically, but most horn players had no conception of it.

From around 1933 onwards, Hawkins's solos were more seamless, in some ways relentless, less inclined to burst into histrionics or special effects because the player knew that there would always be a lot more variations of order and intonation on the *arpeggios* to come before there would be any need to grandstand your way out. Everything he did had a logical melodic flow rare in jazz, which can be inclined to bluster.

When Hawkins returned to the States at the end of the Thirties, after some years in Europe, he recorded a version of 'Body and Soul' that became one of the rare jazz hits. Hawkins responded to this with surprise, maintaining he had been playing the same way for years. But it was a tailor-made smoocher. Hawkins plays virtually all of it in a tender, almost

The saxophone voice that was called 'soundless laughter' – the magic tone of Lester Young.
Young's tenor sound was close to that of a clarinet, and he continued to improvise on the theme rather than the chords.

subdued manner, though some of it is in double-time. There is a brief period verging on excitability in the coda but even that falls back to the smoky tension of the earlier sections. Only in a condensed version of the theme at the outset does Hawkins bother much with the original tune. In all respects but tempo and accent, it has the underpinnings of bebop.

Hawkins's rival for the status of the 1930s' top saxophonist was Lester Young. If Hawkins became a model for a line of modernist saxophonists that included Sonny Rollins and John Coltrane, Young became the model for both the 'cool school' and much of the inspiration of Charlie Parker, one of the least cool of performers.

Young followed Hawkins into the Fletcher Henderson band in 1934. He seemed at first to be a representative of the very traditions of reed-playing in jazz that Hawkins had devoted himself to transforming. Young's sound was light, feathery (it was once described as being like 'soundless laughter'), at times clarinet-like, an instrument he was fond of. He was still absorbed by the song, not the chords. He was not bullish and imposing, he was gentle and restrained. This lack of the heavyweight qualities of Hawkins meant that Young's tenure in the Henderson band was short, and the bandleader eventually found more Hawkins-like musicians (Ben Webster particularly) to replace him with. But Young's style, far from being a pale shadow of what seemed to be the vogue saxophone method of the day, turned into a tributary of jazz at least as significant to the music's overall development.

Young came from Mississippi but was raised in New Orleans, and was nine years Louis Armstrong's junior. His father was a tent show musician, and the boy first played drums with the family business, then saxophones. He acknowledged Beiderbecke's partner, the white saxophonist Frankie Trumbauer, as his primary influence, claiming that his first aim was to try to transfer the light sound of the C-melody saxophone on to the tenor. He also liked Bud Freeman – another white with a good sound, though prone to repetition melodically. Young had played with the Count Basie band on and off, and returned to it after the stretch with Henderson, just as the swing band boom was taking off.

From the end of the Thirties to the end of the war, Young's playing was at its peak, and many of the best examples of it were recorded with various Basie small groups. Very little of Hawkins's preference for substituting more complex chords and looking for tunes with key modulations to add even more variety are audible with Young. He hears the melody in his head, and he hears the scale from which it takes its lead, and will from time to time make unexpected variations on that. The result was that Young was always playing with more economical materials, and relying on his sensitive melodic ear and delicate tone to maintain the variation.

During the late Thirties, Young formed one of the great partnerships in jazz when he recorded a considerable number of sides with Billie Holiday, a performer just as cool, oblique, yet jangling with suppressed emotions as him. Like hers, Young's music could be bright and jaunty at times, or a reduction of music and lyrics to sketches of hushed, sighing sounds. Young's qualities were a kind of vibrant delicacy, a sense of the shape of a solo as good as Armstrong's, or more accurately Beiderbecke's, and a constant reshaping of the melody into wistful new guises.

But coming out of the swing era, it was Hawkins who seemed to have influenced most of the saxophonists. Herschel Evans, Chu Berry and Ben Webster all presented varying faces of this style. Berry had been an altoist originally but took up the tenor on hearing Hawkins. His major swing band jobs were – inevitably – with Fletcher Henderson and later with Cab Calloway, but his death in 1941 truncated a promising career. Berry was not as rich and flowing as Hawkins, less busy in phrasing and luxuriant in ballads, and he had more of a tendency to stay in the upper register. Hershel Evans shared the Hawkins conception, and was a powerful, charismatic player, but his construction of solos didn't have the same inexorable, far-seeing composure. Webster's in the end was the most idiosyncratic and distinctive.

The same age as Lester Young, Ben Webster was another front-rank big-band player who had also worked with Fletcher Henderson, and also, from 1939 to 1943, in the Duke Ellington band. Though Webster was clearly heavily influenced by Hawkins, he stayed closer to the tune. On ballads, he was less inclined than Hawkins to a restless, busy exploration of the possibilities and more likely to reconstruct it as elongated, floating figures frequently ending in a pulsating vibrato or evaporating into puffs of air. At faster speeds, he could be gruff, even grumpy-sounding, but often breaking out into a succession of gravelly phrases driven by a relentless swing. Like Hawkins, Webster was strong on phrasing that ran at odds to the underlying beat to create an impression of pushing the music inexorably before him. The presence of Webster in any band was a hard act to follow, but Ellington successfully attempted it with the hiring of Paul Gonsalves, who had much of Webster's mixture of composure and idiosyncrasy.

Of the other musicians who came to the fore in the 1930s, a name that deserves to be ranked with Hodges on alto – and ultimately, alongside all the major figures on saxophone in jazz – is that of Benny Carter. Born in 1907 in New York, Carter was originally a pianist, then a trumpeter and saxophon-

ist. He began working steadily from the mid-Twenties, and was soon playing in bands led by pianist James P. Johnson, Fletcher Henderson and Duke Ellington. Like Hawkins, Carter's musical knowledge gave him a distinct advantage.

Carter's arranging and composing skills took him to Hollywood in the Fifties, though he periodically continued to perform. One of the most remarkable Carter records is 'Further Definitions', from 1961, in the company of a sprightly Coleman Hawkins, and with younger players like Phil Woods on hand. Carter has an exhilarating tone which if anything has grown more expressive over the years, and his melodic lines have a stately complexity. He has two musical personalities – florid and elegant on saxophone, direct and unfussy on trumpet – and he is a consummate musician.

An influential musician easily overlooked because he specialized in the baritone saxophone – a difficult instrument to sound lyrical on improvisationally – was the Ellington sideman Harry Carney. Carney remained with Ellington all his life (from 1927 to 1974), his massive, imposing sound underpinning the composer's ensemble textures but also reflecting a Hodges-like lyricism and elegance despite the seven-

ABOVE Don Byas, one of the most accomplished and competitive tenor saxophone heroes of the late swing era.

RIGHT Ben Webster, the man who could make puffs of air sound musical. A plush, velvet-toned saxophonist who could nonetheless sound gruff and needled at quick tempos, Webster was influenced by Coleman Hawkins.

league-boot quality of the horn. Carney's sound in solos exhibited a majestic swing and richness of tone that was not to be heard again on the baritone until the emergence of the modernists.

For tenorists, the choice was either the Hawkins camp or the Young camp, and the majority joined the former at first. Buddy Tate continued to play a mixture of swing and rhythm 'n' blues well into the modern era. Lucky Thompson was a musician who bridged swing and bebop, as did Don Byas, who had a fearsome reputation as a driving, competitive soloist. Byas was also the possessor of the fastest technique prior to the bop era, as well as being an unexpectedly sensitive interpreter of ballads. Illinois Jacquet is a wild, exciting, overreaching kind of player, one of the first to extend the range of the tenor saxophone into the 'off-the-instrument' upper limits, though this effect was primarily designed to unleash footstamping in swing audiences rather than explore new musical possibilities.

Also out of the same school but with very different convictions is Benny Golson, who has the expansiveness of the swing musicians even though his inclinations leaned towards bebop. Flip Phillips was in the Jacquet mould, but could play ballads expressively when he took the time, and Charlie Ventura was one of several swing players who saw a commercial potential in a more swing-oriented version of bop in the 1940s, an enterprise he called 'Bop For the People'.

But by the end of the Thirties, a new genius had exploded over the world of jazz. It was the sound of Lester Young that particularly impressed Charlie Parker, the son of a Kansas song-and-dance man. He was given a saxophone by his adoring mother, Addie, although the family lived in poverty. The young Parker taught himself initially, and began to make his way through local bands, eventually joining the New York Jay McShann Orchestra. His solos by that point in his career clearly owe a debt to Lester Young, and somewhat to Johnny Hodges and Benny Carter.

Playing the young saxophonist's 'Lady Be Good' at half speed, according to Parker's biographer Ross Russell, produces an effect almost identical to Young. Russell wrote: 'The effect of "Hootie Blues" sent a shock wave through all those musicians who stumbled on to the B side . . . Those twelve bars were heard as a sermon from the mount. The sinuous line and the stark, pristine architecture of sound revealed a totally new jazz concept . . . It is a Pandora's box of things to come.'

Though the idiom is swing, the saxophonist is evidently attempting not simply to develop a more packed and concentrated plethora of notes even than Hawkins would do, but experimenting with unusual harmonies. Parker himself recalled of his experi-

ments of the period that he thought of improvising with the 'added' notes of chords, the higher intervals – what Russell called 'skimming along the very tops of the chords'. It occurred to him that if he used these as the basis of a new melody line and reconstructed appropriate chords accordingly, he would have the basis of a new music.

Louis Armstrong had liberated the solo voice in jazz. He had taken more liberties with the construction of phrasing and with the relation of the accents to the underlying beat than anyone before him in the music. Parker was to do the same, although the evidence of it was not to become clear to the world until the altoist had left the big-bands that were his training grounds.

He left the McShann band in 1942, and went to New York, where he met Dizzy Gillespie, Thelonious Monk and the other habitués of Minton's Playhouse. These immediately recognized him as a player of vision in a way that none of his other playing partners had ever done. But he was already creating enormous problems for himself as well as achieving enormous insights into the music that obsessed him.

His intake of narcotics and drink astounded those around him. He appeared to be hardly affected by the opinion of others, or by ethical considerations involved in his relationships, whether professional or personal. Though Dizzy Gillespie, who for a while became an inseparable playing partner, introduced him first to the Earl Hines band and then to Billy Eckstine's, he was not to keep these jobs and his erratic behaviour and unreliability made him a risky employee for a full-time commercial outfit.

In 1944 he took a small-band job in a 52nd Street club, The Three Deuces. With that band he made his first mature records, on and off through 1945. The band exploded from loudspeakers of adventurous jazz fans, first in America, then gradually around the world. The music was compressed, the sound diamond-bright and endlessly active. There is a torrent of melodies, counter-rhythms, garrulous trumpet-saxophone dialogues between Parker and Gillespie. It was a revelation, and made Parker's name.

But in 1946 and 1947 Parker's behaviour became more unpredictable as his dependence on heroin increased. He found himself in a mental institution in 1946 and when he returned to New York at the beginning of the following year he was forced to form a new band because Gillespie had run out of patience with him. The 1947 version included the young Miles Davis, sounding unsteady at times and attempting to emulate Dizzy Gillespie with a technique unequal to the job, but nevertheless already displaying a distinctive sense of time and space. Though some of Parker's most dazzling music was

Charlie Parker, whose genius opened the Pandora's box of modern jazz. Parker could think and play faster and more logically than any of his bebop contemporaries, and his audacious phrasing came in part from his use of modified and augmented chords as the basis of new melody. Even in poor health or mental distress, his music continued to soar.

recorded in 1947, it was a time of continuing personal chaos for him. The following year Roach and Davis left, and a young white trumpeter, Red Rodney joined, with Al Haig on piano.

Parker's health held out until March 1955. When he died, a doctor conducting the autopsy assumed him to be 20 years older than he was. During the two years of his most dynamic output, 1945–47, Charlie Parker produced sounds from the saxophone that utterly dumbfounded both fellow saxophonists and the jazz public. Most noticeable in analysis of his solos of that period is that they frequently broke the bar-lines. Where Coleman Hawkins had tended to start and end his phrases on the bar breaks and alter the feel according to where he would scatter accents and emphases, Parker constantly skidded over the road markings so that his phrases would often be of odd lengths, and start in odd positions.

He also constantly varied the note-values so that his solos never sound like a steady unfurling of notes of equal length. Parker could think and play faster

than anyone else in bop at the time, but he didn't barrage the listener with this skill. When they did come, the crackling passages of sixteenth-note runs would come unexpectedly, interrupting the line of the solo and vanishing again. He was also constantly varying the dynamic level from cries to whispers.

Whereas 15 years previously there hadn't been much to go on, aspiring saxophonists were now confronted with considerable riches from which to develop a direction. Coleman Hawkins had virtually defined the swing style as big, dramatic, sensuous, sinewy, loquacious. Lester Young had defined a territory of his own as romantic, spare, graceful, a personal re-definition of melodic improvising. Charlie Parker had taken the clarity of Young's line and the force of Hawkins's attack, and married these with a harmonic audacity and rhythmic unpredictability that neither of the older men could emulate.

After the first flush of bebop, Hawkins's hegemony over saxophone music began to diminish and Young's to increase. Of the more raw-boned school, Gene Ammons was the loudest, fastest and most imposing performer. The son of boogie-woogie pianist Albert Ammons, Gene was a musician who became renowned in the Forties and Fifties for his breakneck two-tenor exchanges with fellow multi-saxist, Sonny Stitt. The latter denied his allegiance to Parker, but his alto playing overwhelmingly testified to it. Ammons's sound had a considerable influence on later R & B players like King Curtis, though curiously his original drive had come from Young.

A group of tenorists started to emerge from the bop revolution who had used Lester Young's conception of phrasing as their springboard. These included Wardell Gray, James Moody and Frank Foster. Moody remains one of the unique saxophone improvisers. His tone is exquisite, his solos are a mixture of wit, passion and drama, and his phrasing on blues often a switchback ride between jagged high sounds and low vibrato.

But if Lester Young had become disoriented and dispirited by the number of musicians who were trying to sound like him – from the swing-era style of 'Vice-Pres' Paul Quinichette with Count Basie, to the soft, autumnal manner of the white performers whose most popular representative was Stan Getz – the domination of Young's sound over the saxophone music of the 1950s was a kind of bitter triumph. The California jazz world (whose most celebrated bandleader was Woody Herman) featured several musicians of this persuasion in Herman's legendary 'Second Herd': Getz, plus Zoot Sims and Herbie Steward.

Getz, Sims, Steward and Guiffre had a Los Angeles band in the mid-Forties, playing arrangements written by Guiffre. Herman heard the outfit and immediately hired them, substituting Serge Chaloff's baritone saxophone for Guiffre. The latter wrote a piece for Herman in 1947 called 'Four Brothers'. The name stuck to both that ensemble within a band, and to the sound they created, one of the most influential in jazz. It was clearly bebop, 'Four Brothers' itself resembling a more sedate rendition of a Charlie Parker uptempo tune. But it had a busy, urbane energy quite different from Parker, and its relaxation, dynamic restraint and lack of bravura led to its becoming one of the inspirations for 'cool jazz'.

Getz's own sound was a hit from the moment the public heard his rendition of 'Early Autumn', the fourth part of a semi-classical suite written as a counterpart to Stravinsky's 'Ebony Concerto' by Woody Herman's inventive arranger Ralph Burns. After solos by the regulars, a 20-year-old Getz closes the piece with a brief statement built around pure, shimmering flute-like sounds and whispering runs,

BELOW *Zoot Sims (left) and Al Cohn (right), two stalwarts of the 1940s' Woody Herman band who inventively adapted Lester Young's light and graceful swing and were perennially popular.*

RIGHT *Lee Konitz, a sensitive and thoughtful performer. Konitz played an important part in the Miles Davis 'Birth of the Cool' 1949 recordings, but continues to grow and listen.*

and those few seconds of recording time were enough to make Getz's reputation.

Although that reputation is built on a romantic ballad style rather than fast playing, Getz has occasionally shown himself more than capable of it, as he did in the company of Dizzy Gillespie ('Diz & Getz') in the 1950s. But throughout his career, Stan Getz has demonstrated his imperious indifference to the crowd-pleasing devices of uptempo playing – not least by adding fragments of whirling runs as afterthoughts or codas in slow pieces where others would build solos around such skills.

With the influence of the Four Brothers' sound and the Miles Davis 'Birth of the Cool' recordings, 'cool jazz' was on its way. The sound of Lester Young was made for it. It found its way into the alto saxophone playing of Lee Konitz and Paul Desmond, the tenor of Warne Marsh and the baritone of Gerry Mulligan. Konitz was a student of pianist Lennie Tristano (see pages 23 and 74) and from the pianist he learned an even, uninflected style that was part of Tristano's war on bar lines, and an alertness to improvising on constant key changes.

Desmond's career was made with the Dave Brubeck group, but was often masked by the pianist's thumping block chord techniques and obsessions with complicated metre. Beneath all this, Desmond was a Konitz-like performer but with an even more feathery tone and shy, almost anxious attack, frequently compelled by the desire to explore a very small quantity of musical material at a time, as if concerned not to waste valuable resources.

Konitz was probably the member of that particular grouping who was most fascinated by experimentation with different improvising situations – a curiosity he has retained to the present day. Desmond and Marsh were the most fragile, porcelain-like of these musicians. And the most vibrant, passionate and possibly the most expansive of all of them was the Los Angeles-born altoist, Art Pepper.

Pepper was influenced by Lester Young and Charlie Parker, but also by Konitz and Zoot Sims. He had a searing, sometimes desperate sound, and a manner of introducing solos with an irresistibly magnetic gradualness and drama. Although he was entirely capable of hard-bop technicalities, he preferred a broken, hesitant line to a scything legato one. The result was one of the most moving and distinctive saxophone sounds in post-war jazz. But he could certainly play 'hot' when the mood took him. On an album like 'Art Pepper Meets the Rhythm Section' (a recording with the Miles Davis rhythm team of 1957) he is stung by the needling drumming of Philly Joe Jones into some tumultuous blowing on 'Straight Life' and an audacious accelerating and dragging of the beat on a quick version of 'The Man I Love'.

One of the idiom's little known but highly gifted exponents in Europe was a Scots musician called Bobby Wellins. He exhibited much of the inspiration for careful editing, soft, petal-like tone, and the imposing of personality through minimal materials of Paul Desmond, or even Getz. Wellins demonstrated this resoundingly on the tune 'Starless and Bible Black' from the British pianist Stan Tracey's 'Under Milk Wood' suite in the mid-Sixties.

Parker's influence nevertheless persisted, not just in the adapted sound of the cool school, but also in a manner closer to his own method of delivery – notably with Lou Donaldson, Cannonball Adderley, Jackie McLean, Phil Woods, Frank Strozier, and Charles McPherson. And on the tenor, there were two towering descendants of both Parker's line and Coleman Hawkins's – Sonny Rollins and Dexter Gordon; while there was a variety of less innovative but engaging practitioners in Johnny Griffin, Hank Mobley, Joe Henderson, Sam Rivers and George Coleman.

Dexter Gordon emerged from the Lionel Hampton band of 1940–43. His sound had the monumental impact of Hawkins (Gordon compounded this imposing effect by being six foot four (193 cm) and handling the tenor as if it were a toy). And he combined this with the lazily-spun melodic web and fondness for long notes of Lester Young and, later, the innovations of Charlie Parker. Gordon soon joined the famous Billy Eckstine Band, where he found himself alongside Dizzy Gillespie, Gene Ammons, and another powerful Parker-like saxophonist, the altoist and sometime tenorist Sonny Stitt.

Gordon recorded some legendary two-tenor chases with Wardell Gray, but his powerful style didn't suit the 1950s taste for cool music and his popularity was eclipsed until the Sixties. Gordon's sound is hard and has much of Parker's almost arrogant spraying of dense clusters of notes. But he has never been as harmonically preoccupied as Parker. His vibrato is dormant except as a spinechilling special effect, and his solos are massively interlocking chunks of sound that amount to constructions as substantial and granite-like as anything in the often ephemeral canon of jazz. Fittingly, Gordon – who had once been a part-time actor in the Broadway jazz-life production of *The Connection* – imposingly played the part of the Lester Young–Bud Powell character, Dale Thompson, in the 1987 cult film, *Round Midnight*.

Sonny Rollins continues to dominate the jazz scene as Miles Davis does, still playing marathon concerts although past his 60th year. An alto player originally, and a childhood friend of Thelonious Monk, Rollins had started out by attempting to merge the methods of the 'jump' players, swing, and Charlie Parker's methods of phrasing. He switched to tenor and

joined Miles Davis in 1951.

Six years later, at a creative peak in the years 1957–58, Rollins began to define the tenor sound that became such a cornerstone of the movement soon to be known as 'hard bop'. Sentiment, softness or delicacy were driven from the music. It was gravelly and rugged in tone; it used themes skeletal to the point of indecency; it exhibited the harmonic understanding of Hawkins without being tied to a 'chord-progression' method of improvising. As often as not, Rollins would blow on the melody, and then on sub-melodies he has concocted out of the original one, or ones at odds to it. His improvising tended to go on at considerable length.

Rollins's sound can be sour, but his control of the early-jazz art of arriving at a pitch through stealth or what initially just seems like a mistake is second-nature. He is a master of the rhythmically unexpected (his solos constantly begin and end in odd places), and he can appear to extract every nuance and twist from a song. A multiplicity of choruses was a characteristic of hard bop. It was a method taken up even more assiduously by John Coltrane.

If there are two names that have become virtually synonymous with avant-garde jazz they are John Coltrane and Ornette Coleman. Coltrane began as a Parkerish altoist, then became a Gordonish tenorist, though Sonny Rollins's more broken and idiosyncratic phrasing probably interested him too. By the time he had passed through his first stint with Miles Davis and performed his highly educative stretch with Thelonious Monk in 1957, his sound was well on the way to being the trademark that innumerable saxophone players have tried to copy since.

It is based on chords – but on such a refinement of the bebop notion of using chord substitutions that the new melodic lines made possible by the extra notes in Coltrane's alternatives intertwine so densely and at such speed that they are barely distinguishable. This implacable effect is what led the style to be dubbed 'sheets of sound'. Coltrane was not just making the straight substitution of a more complex chord for the one originally written in a tune. He was making substitutions of several chords for every one, and in attempting to pack in all the possible improvised lines 'liberated' by the extra chord voicings, he was having to play at breakneck speed and virtually without pauses.

Though the tone had something in common with the dryness and muscularity of Sonny Rollins, the phraseology was the diametric opposite. Rollins

The clout of Coleman Hawkins, the speed of Charlie Parker, the fragmented phrasing and subversiveness of Thelonious Monk and a strong flavour of the Caribbean meet in Sonny Rollins. Rollins is a master of surprise.

would expound, pause, guffaw, hesitate, hold forth, and disappear into guttural, grumbling sounds. Coltrane would seem to play *all* the time, a torrent of notes made possible by his obsessive study of advanced harmonic theory. They didn't always fit the rhythm, so Coltrane would drift wildly away from the rhythm but generally return unerringly to it. It was a curious, mesmerizing, manic kind of virtuosity. By 1958 it had taken him back into the Miles Davis band again – to record some memorable albums like 'Kind of Blue' and 'Milestones', and gained him a reputation as a tenorist comfortably equal to that of Sonny Rollins.

Ornette Coleman came to public notice in 1959, through the recording date he had secured with Lester Koenig, the adventurous head of a small L.A. label called Contemporary Records. Listening to Ornette Coleman's early recordings today makes it difficult to reconstruct the original controversy. He played tunes (often very moving and bluesy ones); the music swung hard – not least because two great and economical bop-style drummers, Billy Higgins and Ed Blackwell, were often involved; and the saxophonist's own sound seemed to combine much of the mobility of Charlie Parker with the rough and expressive tonality of very early jazz musicians. It did not, however, proceed on a conventional tramline of chord changes. A British critic, Victor Schonfield, wrote in the liner notes to a Coleman album of the mid-Sixties; 'His lovely tone is essentially the sound of jazz, like those of Johnny Dodds, Bubber Miley, Lester Young and Charlie Parker.'

Coleman's approach to improvising was a matter of constant variety. Once listeners got past the unexpectedly exultant panache with which he delivered off-pitch, squalling and crying sounds that had not been so centrally expressed by a jazz soloist for years, the inventiveness of his solos became spectacularly evident. A flurry of abrasive, braying sounds delivered as a run might suddenly end in a jolting, declamatory honk. There might then be a silence before a sidelong, mischievous melody would creep back in, played at half the volume and in quite a different mood, and in the course of this Coleman might sardonically quote a fragment of a standard. There might then be a louder descending passage, sounding like a cackle of laughter.

Coleman's 'Free Jazz' explorations on record in 1960 (see page 29) established a loose, reactive ensemble-playing method that was much copied, or at least adapted. By the time that Coleman was making 'Free Jazz', John Coltrane was making ready to leave Miles Davis for the second time and launch a career of his own. Coleman was about to return to relative obscurity for several years because his music alienated many, and because his relationships with the music business were prickly. But Coltrane didn't need to establish his credibility with anyone; the years with Miles Davis and with Monk had done that. On two albums in 1959–60 ('Coltrane Jazz' and 'Giant Steps') the saxophonist made a clear statement of where he had been and where he was going.

On 'Giant Steps' there were tunes that were based on modes, not chords – in other words, cycles of

LEFT *Since the 1960s, John Coltrane has been a guru to musicians and to much of the music-loving public alike. A single-minded and deeply spiritual man, Coltrane produced torrential music from a blend of his constant studies of theory and the desire to create a devotional form of jazz. Today's young musicians continue to pore over his methods.*

RIGHT *If John Coltrane introduced formidable complexities into modern jazz soloing, Ornette Coleman sought to simplify it. He rejected chords, improvising in a more freely-associative way, with sound somewhere between Charlie Parker and a rough-and-ready rhythm 'n' blues saxophonist. Coleman's methods were called primitive, and rejected at first. Time has proved his tunes to be enduring and his inventiveness undimmed.*

scales. This method had already surfaced with Miles Davis – 'Milestones' and 'Kind of Blue' – and in Coltrane's case had come to him both from his constant researches into musical theory and the rapidly developing interest in the East, where modal playing was more common.

Coltrane now had a different basis from which to begin his odysseys into improvisation, and already an astonishing technique on the saxophone. The combination of these elements led him to take his journey into the field of polytonality – sometimes using the notes of the scale he was principally playing in, sometimes introducing notes from another one. By the time 'My Favourite Things' appeared in late 1960, these investigations had borne considerable fruit. But far from alienating the jazz public by

experimentation, the record became a hit. The security this development bought Coltrane allowed him to move steadily forward. He knew the free-jazz movement was gathering momentum. Though in many ways it differed sharply from his own notion of freeing himself from the past by ever more elaborate learning, its impulses were similar to his.

Though the membership of his own quartet had by now steadied (Elvin Jones on drums, Jimmy Garrison on bass, McCoy Tyner on piano), he worked from time to time with other players who were at the same stage in the exploration of freedom, or even further out. One was Eric Dolphy, the alto saxophonist and bass clarinettist. Dolphy and Coltrane had known each other since the mid-Fifties. Dolphy had begun, almost inevitably, as a Parkerish

altoist, and made a name for himself in the Chico Hamilton group. The fire and passion of his playing and his occupation of the outer reaches of the horn's range had suggested that bebop would not hold him.

With Charles Mingus from 1960 on, Dolphy suggested that, had early death not intervened (in 1964), he might have been as prominent and creative a figure in the New Jazz as Coltrane and Coleman were. His alto playing tends to be at the upper end of the horn, and his sound vocalized, expressive and sometimes pained. On 'Out to Lunch', his most famous recording, these qualities are evident in the title track. On this, Dolphy's solo is a mixture of furious flurries, ascending fluttering runs that end on squeaky high notes, single-note statements that skip wide intervals, and periods of more leisurely reflection that sound like Ornette Coleman on a slow tune.

Coltrane's search also located two other avant-garde saxophonists. One was Farrell 'Pharoah' Sanders, a tenorist of the school once dubbed – pejoratively, but accurately – the 'rubbed-balloon'

LEFT *Eric Dolphy, an audacious and restlessly searching reed player of the 1960s' avant-garde*

ABOVE *Albert Ayler took free-jazz back to the sound of New Orleans marches, and to gospel.*

style of horn playing. Where Dolphy occupied a bridge between orthodox tonality and atonal playing, Sanders was almost exclusively devoted to the outer limits by the time he joined Coltrane. Archie Shepp, however, had been born in less tempestuous climates.

Shepp had been a rhythm-and-blues tenorist like Ornette Coleman. He briefly joined the pianist Cecil Taylor at the beginning of the Sixties, and his saxophone playing now seems clearly to stand in a direct line from Coleman Hawkins and Ben Webster, though influenced by the prolixity of hard bop and some of the extremities of sound unleashed by the avant-garde.

Like Archie Shepp, Albert Ayler was a free-jazz saxophonist who began to command attention in the middle of the Sixties and who had served an apprenticeship in R & B bands. Like both Shepp and Ornette Coleman, Ayler was concerned to restore a simplicity and directness to jazz horn playing in which the infrastructure of the music dominates the outcome much less. Ayler's sound can have a chilling, ghostly, gale-in-the-chimney effect, with a reverberating vibrato, wild swings across the register and a variety of squeals, honks and wails, but he did not uniformly endorse free-jazz. Some of his later recordings leant on formats like New Orleans funeral marches, gospel and even rock 'n' roll. Ayler may have been an enfant terrible of the 1960s, but his antecedents were Lester Young and Sidney Bechet.

Musicians like John Gilmore, Dewey Redman (the son of 1920s orchestra leader Don Redman), David Murray, George Adams and Chico Freeman have all continued to develop the ideas of that time, often with a virtuosity comparable to the highest flights of harmonically complex bebop. Redman particularly made a place for himself, by becoming a regular musical partner of both Ornette Coleman and Don Cherry, though his playing was a distinctive mixture of gravelly directness and the melodic composure of a player like Hank Mobley.

And even in John Coltrane, the most technically advanced of all of them, who appeared to have devoted a good part of his musical life to increasing the complexity that bebop had introduced rather than reducing it, the voices of the early jazz players were constant echoes in the back of his head. Joachim Berendt recalls Coltrane frequently asking for copies of Sidney Bechet's European sessions to be mailed to him in the late Fifties, and the veteran saxophonist was undoubtedly a significant influence on the younger one's decision to take up the soprano. In any event, after the success of 'My Favourite Things', a soprano exercise, the instrument began to enjoy a boom.

Coltrane's work on the soprano, like Don Cherry's on the pocket trumpet and then on 'exotic'

instruments, helped open jazz up to the music of the wider world. This was aided by the fact that Coltrane's sound drew from, and continually suggested, Indian and Middle Eastern wind instruments.

A soprano player called Steve Lacy had used the instrument in modern jazz prior to Coltrane. He had been a New Orleans player, and Bechet influenced him in Bechet's own idiom. In the 1950s, Lacy made an abrupt switch from early jazz to the avant-garde, playing with uncompromising experimenters like Cecil Taylor. But Lacy also developed a good

ABOVE *A soprano saxophonist who began under Sidney Bechet's spell, Steve Lacy emerged from it to work fruitfully with modernists like Thelonious Monk and Cecil Taylor.*

RIGHT *Stan Getz, possessor of one of the most exquisite tones in jazz saxophone playing and the music's foremost balladeer in the opinion of many. Even Coltrane quoted him as an influence.*

relationship with Thelonious Monk. Latterly, the saxophonist has moved between Monk tributes and the farthest reaches of the European avant-garde, and is a crafty purveyor of both dissonance and a kind of squeaky, mouse-in-the-skirting lyricism.

The soprano also began to be used in jazz by tenorists on the avant-garde who were getting falsetto effects from overblowing, but without much control. But of all the musicians of the Sixties and Seventies who had a powerful influence in jazz, Wayne Shorter became the most impressive sopranoist. Shorter performed with Art Blakey's Jazz Messengers for a while, but joined Miles Davis in the mid-Sixties.

In 1969, he recorded on soprano for the first time, and played some ringingly beautiful solos on 'In a Silent Way'. Shorter's soprano sound was clear, even shrill, but swept through the registers in a manner that seemed to enlarge the stage set by the fundamentally limited materials in operation at this point in Davis's investigations of rock. Since this period, Shorter's contribution has been somewhat eclipsed in the storms of sound awash in the successful fusion band Weather Report, but it has emerged again with some small band recordings of his own, in which his imagination as a composer also gets a chance to unfurl.

While the free scene was gathering momentum,

LEFT *Easily underestimated as a sideshow act, and one of the finest all-round entertainers ever to be a jazz musician, multi-instrumentalist Rahsaan Roland Kirk was nevertheless unswervingly dedicated to furthering what he called 'black classical music'.*

RIGHT *Brother of trumpeter Wynton, Branford Marsalis is influenced by Wayne Shorter, Ornette Coleman and Coltrane – and like many young 1980s' musicians, he has sought to express his respect for the past, reinterpreting standards, the work of Charles Mingus, and the classical repertoire. He has also toured with a band led by rock singer Sting.*

that inspired protector and nurturer of Lester Young classicism, Stan Getz, came dramatically back into style. In 1961, largely through the inclination of guitarist, Charlie Byrd, and his travels to Brazil, a succession of hit records were made using Brazilian elements wedded to the breathy, whispering, tenor style of cool jazz. They made Getz's reputation all over again. After the fuss died down in the mid-Sixties, Getz's style toughened – to the dismay of some of his fans, who felt he was making inappropriate concessions to modernism and the fragmentary, angular attack of players like Sonny Rollins. But the saxophonist was disinclined to stay in one place, even if it was a lucrative place. Partly he may have realized that a lucrative place doesn't stay like that forever.

Both Zoot Sims and Al Cohn continued to tour the world, playing clubs in their freewheeling, jaunty and effortlessly musical manner. Hard bop saxophonists like Dexter Gordon and Johnny Griffin enjoyed a comeback, Gordon to some extent triggering a trend with a spectacular return to New York in

the late Seventies.

An extraordinary and unclassifiable musician who bridged all these areas and managed to be one of the best-loved and most entertaining performers into the bargain, was the multi-instrumentalist, Rahsaan Roland Kirk. Kirk was liable to be treated as a sideshow despite his protestations that he played 'black classical music', because he could be enjoyed on the basis of his remarkable multi-instrumental playing (not just as a master of several instruments, but several instruments played at the same time). Beneath it all, he was a hard-bopper, and his long, thrashing tenor saxophone forays, given added momentum by advanced breathing techniques, could generate feverish excitement in clubs.

The younger generation of saxophonists has been able to beachcomb among all these styles. Some went way back, all the way into swing. The most famous of these is Scott Hamilton from Providence, Rhode Island. Young saxophonists of the neo-bop school notably include Bob Berg, Dave Schnitter, Branford

Marsalis, the latter a young man as likely to record the New Orleans tune 'Royal Garden Blues' as a theme in the 1960s Coltrane manner. And from a mixture of Coltrane and fusion music came Gato Barbieri, Mike Brecker, Wilton Felder and Ronnie Laws.

More recently, the emergence of black pop forms like rap and funk have encouraged some players who could easily have sustained a reputation within the currently fashionable idiom of neo-bop. Perhaps the most talented of these players is the 31-year-old New Yorker, Steve Coleman. Coming to prominence in a highly sophisticated band that blended bop and a streamlined version of the earthiness of Charles Mingus led by bassist Dave Holland, Steve Coleman's own recordings lead his impassioned, Ornette-like alto to situate itself in surroundings mostly suggestive of 1980s New York street life.

As we saw in the opening chapter, the free music scene not only introduced a wider range of instrumental techniques in the home of jazz, but elsewhere in the world as well. All the earlier idioms of jazz – New Orleans, swing, bebop – had come complete with their own highly identifiable trademarks. Authenticity in these borrowed styles seemed possible only through a thorough absorption of the recognizable features. Free music allowed performers everywhere to take what they had inherited apart and rebuild it in the image of their own cultures. And the American reed-player who was most consistently interested in forging links between the original sources of the music and the new contributions has been Anthony Braxton, who has already been briefly considered.

Braxton quotes white 'cool' players like Lee Konitz and Paul Desmond as influences on his early saxophone playing, but from the mid-Sixties these spacious methods blended with the more heated sound of the avant-garde. He also revealed an insight into bebop that enabled him not merely to pay homage to it but to extend its language in a manner that was nostalgic and experimental at the same time. Braxton is an inspiration to those tempted to practise drastic surgery on an existing idiom.

This has led both to the emergence of a number of powerful individualists from outside America or the Afro-American tradition. German, Peter Brotzmann not only exhibits one of the loudest sounds in all jazz, but also one of the most brutally dramatic. His inspiration has come down from Coltrane and Pharoah Sanders, and when suitably galvanized by a sufficiently thunderous rhythm (he often plays with the 'punk jazz' or 'no wave' drummer Ronald Shannon Jackson) his improvisations can unnervingly resemble the advance of a herd of maddened elephants.

The Dutch reed player Willem Breuker is of a quite different persuasion. Breuker's music is composed, ironic, and draws as much from Kurt Weill as it does from Ornette Coleman. Evan Parker, a British tenorist and soprano player, has explored the territory embarked on by John Coltrane in producing harmonics and overblown notes on the saxophones. Unaccompanied solos by Parker now include as many as three simultaneous lines: squeals, squawks, cluckings and ticking rhythmic figures pulling and pushing at each other over drone-like underpinnings, the whole lot often played for fifteen minutes or more without pause. Parker is a master of the technique of circular breathing.

BELOW *A Coltrane-influenced saxophonist, Mike Brecker has operated in many spheres of jazz but particularly fruitfully in the brand of sophisticated fusion associated with guitarist Pat Metheny.*

RIGHT *British saxophonist Evan Parker has worked in free-music for most of his career but occasionally appears in more jazzy contexts. He is a master of the art of playing contrasting lines simultaneously.*

European free music has produced its major romantic figure too – the Norwegian saxophonist Jan Garbarek. Garbarek began as a Coltrane fan in the 1960s, but diverted the resonant, soulful intonation into a spacious, unhurried, programmatic music that constantly suggests a film-score for a story set in the fjords.

Another European whose talent for linking Coltrane's legacy with local folklore almost rivals Garbarek's is Briton John Surman. In his case the connecting point has frequently been British folk music. Surman mostly uses the soprano and electronics these days, but he emerged in the Sixties as a baritone saxophonist who had genuinely extended the potential of the instrument as mapped out by Carney, Serge Chaloff and Gerry Mulligan. Surman successfully developed a technique for adapting Coltrane's tenor style to the heavier horn.

Alan Skidmore, a contemporary of Surman's, has also been prominent in Europe over the past decade for more direct representations of the style of the classic Coltrane quartet. And latterly in England a group of dramatic saxophonists are operating generally in the pre-free Coltrane manner. The most celebrated of these performers so far are Londoners Courtney Pine and Steve Williamson.

CHAPTER TEN

GUITAR HEROES

> ❛Jimi Hendrix spoke of the guitar
> as his lover ❜
>
> JOACHIM BERENDT

In jazz, guitars or banjos have had an ensemble role which was more or less the extent of their contribution. There is photographic evidence that a guitarist was featured in Buddy Bolden's band for a while, as early as the 1890s. But the more penetrative sound of the banjo was better suited to New Orleans outfits since the combined voicings of a trumpet, trombone and clarinet, probably backed by enthusiastic drumming, would almost certainly be sufficient to render a guitarist's work inaudible.

Pat Metheny, a jazz fan from childhood who has become one of the best-known guitarists on the bridge between jazz and pop.

New Orleans musicians Johnny St. Cyr and Lonnie Johnson were two of the most notable early practitioners – and the first evidence of a parting of the ways about how these instruments could be married to jazz. St. Cyr was an ensemble player who worked with Armstrong and Morton. His undramatic but incisive chordal work behind the soloists added a solidity to the overall sound that anchored the swirling kite-flying of the idiom's front-line contrapuntal playing. Johnson was already embarking on a more independent role.

Lonnie Johnson was really the father of the jazz guitar sound. He was forced to be a part-time musician in his early career, working in foundries and tyre factories around Cleveland. But he developed as a successful guitarist and singer in the Thirties and Forties. His sound was distinctive, partly because he doubled up the treble strings to gain an effect like a 12-stringed instrument. He played finger-style, but flat-picked as well, and his improvised lines were long and highly imaginative, particularly on blues.

Johnson and Italian-American guitarist Eddie Lang recorded a number of duets – some of them featuring King Oliver on trumpet – that effectively put the notion of single-line jazz guitar improvisa-tion on the map. Lang was the son of a guitar maker (his sister also played the instrument) and he was taught violin as a child, switching to banjo when he began to get professional work in the Twenties. Lang was present on legendary Bix Beiderbecke perfor-mances like 'I'm Comin' Virginia', and his career boomed in the following decade when he worked both as a singer and as accompanist to Bing Crosby – but he died having his tonsils removed in 1933.

Lang's harmonic knowledge was advanced, his tone robust, and his single-line figures intricate,

LEFT *Gypsy guitarist Django Rheinhardt, one of the few early European jazz musicians to gain an international reputation. His playing was impulsive, exuberant and confident, and he approached most of his playing as if on his last gig.*

ABOVE *Playing a solo was virtually sacreligious to him, but Count Basie's Freddie Green is a model of sympathetic rhythmic accompaniment.*

RIGHT *Eddie Durham, Jimmy Lunceford's guitarist – the man who used piano mikes to amplify his instrument, and thereby changed the destiny of the guitar forever.*

logical and full of unexpected intervals, slurs and harmonics. All this fire-power made him a better improviser than his frequent partner Johnson, though he was not as effective on blues.

St. Cyr's rhythmic style, on the other hand, influenced Count Basie's guitarist over many years, Freddie Green. Green made such a virtue of utterly dependable yet lively and vigorous four-to-the-bar chord playing that the rhythm section of Count Basie's finest bands would have been substantially weakened without him, even considering the presence of a drummer such as Jo Jones. Eddie Condon, a white musician of considerable influence in the 'Chicago school' was also an excellent rhythm guitarist, though not in Green's league.

Following in the Johnson/Lang mould came Teddy Bunn, George Van Eps, Dick McDonough and Carl Kress. But it was the Belgian gypsy guitarist Django Rheinhardt who gave the development of the instrument its next spectacular shot in the arm. With the famous Quintet du Hot Club de France – three guitars, violin and double bass – Rheinhardt's playing was a revelation not just to other guitarists but to players on any instrument. He experimented with octave runs, which gave his sound a rich, chiming quality. He launched into solos – regardless of tempo – with an intensity and indifference to slow build-ups that is suggestive of Charlie Parker in its blazing confidence, if not in idiom. All this was being done with only two useful fingers on his fretting hand, Rheinhardt having been injured in a caravan fire when he was 18.

Rheinhardt was triumphant in small groups. In the Thirties the fashion was for size, and size overwhelmed the acoustic guitar player. Guitarist Eddie Durham, also a trombonist, composer and arranger, and a member of the Jimmie Lunceford Orchestra, used a form of electric amplification with that band in 1935. Floyd Smith, a player of Hawaiian guitar who worked with the Andy Kirk band, also used an amplifier. These experiments changed the sound of jazz guitar forever.

A means of making the instrument audible in the big-band era was an inevitable development. Durham managed it by using piano mikes initially, as Stuff Smith was doing for his violin. The guitarist complained of the technical difficulties – too much volume and the instrument sounded like an organ, or the clean rhythmic sound was obliterated in a blur. But it was Charlie Christian, a young Texan musician who joined the Benny Goodman band in 1939, who combined the innovations of amplification and the harmonic and rhythmic breakthroughs of bebop to make the guitar a front-line jazz instrument of equal status with all the others.

Christian was a superb improviser. As his experience and his reputation grew with Goodman, Chris-

tian increasingly substituted alternative chord constructions by stacking the basic triads with rarely used superimpositions – elevenths and thirteenths at the top end, the material that Charlie Parker was using to expand his range of available notes for improvisation. Like early Lester Young, Christian was fond of a smooth legato style, but he was varying the raw material by a different means: making the resolutions of phrases happen in unexpected parts of the bar. This contribution had a substantial impact on the ideas of the young beboppers working the new music out at Minton's Playhouse and Monroe's Uptown House (see pages 18–21) and the young guitarist's music would undoubtedly have loosened up even further but for his death from tuberculosis in 1942.

A group of guitarists intrigued by bebop and inspired by Christian emerged in the 1940s and early

ABOVE *The guitarist's guitarist – Tal Farlow, from Carolina, who blends Lester Young's long melodic lines with the speed and dynamism of bop.*

RIGHT *Eddie Durham experimented with electric guitars, Charlie Christian brought them to maturity in the short span of his career. A star soloist with Benny Goodman, Christian was also one of the founders of bebop.*

Fifties. These included Billy Bauer, Bill DeArango, Tal Farlow, Barney Kessel and Jimmy Raney. All these musicians developed Christian's concept of allowing the electric amplification to let the guitar take its place among the horns. The lines these musicians played thus echoed those of the saxophonists, and Farlow in particular became an object of study by other practitioners. The Carolina-born guitarist, a regular partner of the vibes player Red Norvo, combined the melodic ideas of the Charlie Christian/Lester Young axis with the Charlie Parker one, a combination made possible by Farlow's mastery of a technique that probably exceeded Christian's, and by the natural blessing of huge hands capable of bridging great distances on the fingerboard.

Of the guitarists that followed the first group of beboppers – Kenny Burrell, Jim Hall, Charlie Byrd and Wes Montgomery – it is Montgomery that acquired the biggest reputation and became the most significant influence on practitioners of the instrument to come.

Both Burrell and Hall have made their mark, the former in particular an excellent blues and hard bop player, and the latter – after Montgomery's early death – to some extent taking his place as an improviser of lyricism, swing and streams of new melody, though Hall has always done it with a spare, hushed style.

Byrd, a classically trained performer who uses a Spanish concert guitar, performs an attractive blend of rich chords and elegant solo lines that never stray far from them, and his moment came for wide recognition with the success of the 'jazz samba' collaborations with Stan Getz and Astrud Gilberto in the early Sixties.

But Montgomery burst on to the jazz world of the 1950s like the meteor that Charlie Christian had been. An Indianapolis musician who rarely travelled far, Montgomery was a long time being discovered, though he had played an impressive stint with the Lionel Hampton band. His sound was unique, because in addition to the soft, bass-toned amplification used by most jazz guitarists at the time, Montgomery used his thumb to pluck the notes – an innovation developed out of trying to practise quietly to avoid upsetting his neighbours.

Montgomery's soft sound, melodiousness and

ABOVE RIGHT *In the mid-1960s the soft, muffled jazz guitar sound was replaced by a more excitable, metallic tone drawn from rock. John McLaughlin, a Briton who went to the States to join Miles Davis, was one architect of the merger.*

LEFT *Quiet man of the jazz guitar, Jim Hall was dubbed the thinking fan's guitarist 30 years ago, and his playing has retained its mixture of hushed, velvet-glove delicacy and bluesy swing.*

RIGHT *The man with the golden thumb, Wes Montgomery – the most relaxed, swinging and fertile guitar improvisor since Charlie Christian and a strong influence on many younger performers, notably Pat Metheny.*

continual swing – he imparted more rhythmic drive than almost any guitarist in jazz – made him attractive to the record business. The last years of his short life saw him making some highly commercial records in which the purr of his chord and octave playing replaced most of the slashing single-line runs full of perfectly formed and rounded notes that had made him such a devastating member of small groups.

Wes Montgomery died in 1968 of a heart attack at the age of 43. He lived long enough to hear the beginnings of that expansion of rock 'n' roll that began to include extensive use of improvisation and the use of the guitar for much more than simply rhythm playing and short instrumental breaks. The soft, sometimes subdued tone of the jazz guitar up to that point (musicians usually used the bass tone control full up, or an instrument with only a bass pickup, which produced a sound as if the guitar was being plucked by someone wearing gloves) was superseded overnight by the wild, wailing sound of amplification with increasingly sophisticated tonal modification.

Jimi Hendrix, an American R & B guitarist living

in England, was a powerful and often moving performer with this technology, and would inventively use the feedback from his own amplifier to release a range of swooping, yearning, crying sounds that had never been possible with a guitar before.

The R & B 'boom' brought back to public notice older blues guitarists using a sparer style but with a harder sound than jazz musicians. These included B.B. King, Albert King and Buddy Guy. As a consequence, jazz-based musicians began to take on the musical – and commercial – possibilities of sounding somewhere between jazz and 1960s rock. A group of highly skilled players emerged with this more metallic, bluesier sound – like John Abercrombie, John Scofield, and (in his pre-Indian music career) John McLaughlin.

McLaughlin is a British expatriate who went to the States in the late Sixties to work with Miles Davis. He combines superlative technique (he is a long-time admirer of Django Rheinhardt), a kind of classicized

ABOVE *Out of the Ornette Coleman stable came James 'Blood' Ulmer, a guitarist who blends funk with Coleman's improvising.*

LEFT *Sonny Sharrock, the New York musician who invented a version of punk jazz before anyone invented punk. He favoured wild, splintering chords and dramatic, sometimes chilling sound effects.*

RIGHT *Comfortable interpreting composers from Ellington to McCoy Tyner, Emily Remler's reputation was made when she was barely 20. She has performed as a leader and in partnership with fellow-guitarist Larry Coryell, but also worked with singers Nancy Wilson and Astrud Gilberto.*

blues, and an ability to improvise modally that made his lines far more unexpected and ambiguous than the chord-change players who had gone before, however talented.

Scandinavian guitarist Terje Rypdal used bugs to the extent that his instrument began at times to sound like a violin section. American Pat Metheny has made inspired melodic use of technology and blended his affection for Wes Montgomery with clear country-music inflections.

Ralph Towner and Egberto Gismonti have developed the art of the jazz-derived acoustic solo recital to a stage that easily rivals the guitar's use in formal concert music. Emily Remler, a 31-year-old New Yorker who counts her inspirations as Hendrix, Montgomery, Farlow and Charlie Byrd, is a remarkable technician whose music has both breadth of view and an attractive lyricism.

At the other side of the park, with the avant-garde, Sonny Sharrock and James Blood Ulmer in the States and Derek Bailey in Britain have revolutionized the playing of the instrument. Sharrock gets a sound from the guitar like a car crash, but beneath the splintering, percussive sound of his playing there is a blues feeling that reaches back to the very beginnings of jazz.

Ulmer, who has worked extensively with Ornette Coleman, blends jazz improvisation with funk and constructs solos of whirling cycles of notes built around repetitive dance rhythms. Bailey, originally a bebopper turned Coltrane admirer, began in the 1960s to incorporate all kinds of unexpected devices into his technique – elements of the serial music of Schoenberg, use of electronics to produce pointillistic sounds that suddenly gleam like stars, to be instantly replaced by scrabbling, scuffling sounds played behind the bridge of the instrument. At the sharp end of jazz, and the bridge where it meets contemporary and avant-garde straight music, Bailey has become a pace-setter for guitarists venturing into this risky but frequently illuminating musical world, where musical cliches are purged as if they were bacteria.

CHAPTER ELEVEN

VIOLINS, VIBES AND FLUTES

> ‘ It don't mean a thing if it
> ain't got that Swing ’
>
> DUKE ELLINGTON

The Violin

Like the guitarist, the early jazz violinist experienced at the outset a simple practical problem: in any ensemble with horns and drums, particularly if they're being played for all they're worth, the sound of a violin is quickly swamped. The first prominent jazz performer on violin was Giuseppe 'Joe' Venuti, born around the turn of the century in Milan and raised in Pennsylvania by Italian immigrant parents. Venuti, who worked extensively with an Italian

Eighty-one years old and still swinging, Stephane Grappelli has performed with partners ranging from Django Rheinhardt to Yehudi Menuhin.

violinist-turned-guitarist called Salvatore 'Eddie Lang' Massaro, was a musician of immense vitality and extrovert charm. His melodic lines were a constant effervescent flow, peppered with gritty chords and runs that seemed endlessly to bubble in the mid-register, postponing their inevitable ascent.

The best known of all jazz violinists is Paris-born Stephane Grappelli, Django Rheinhardt's most famous partner. At the end of the 1920s, Grappelli was a pianist and violinist performing popular music in Paris. By the mid-Thirties Rheinhardt and Grappelli had united a developing interest in jazz to form the nucleus of one of the most celebrated of all European jazz bands – the Quintet du Hot Club de France.

ABOVE Vitality, momentum and power. Milan-born Joe Venuti was one of the foremost early jazz violinists.

LEFT Stuff Smith, the man who first amplified the violin, and substituted grit and brusque charm for violin refinement. Impresario Norman Granz even paired him with Dizzy Gillespie, and Smith proved he had a shrewd understanding of bebop.

RIGHT Jean Luc Ponty learned from the work of John Coltrane as much as from Grappelli or Stuff Smith. He later became a popular exponent of jazz-rock.

Grappelli improved steadily from the 1930s as he loosened the grip of his classical training, and developed an infectious swing and a constantly good-humoured and affable feel in his playing. He still sounds elegant and leisurely into his eighties.

The violinist who most relentlessly shook by the neck the refined violin style which most trained players exhibited as second nature was the American Hezekiah Leroy 'Stuff' Smith. Smith was the first violinist to use electric amplification, adapting a piano mike, as guitarist Eddie Durham did. He was also the first to develop bebop phrasing.

French violinist Jean-Luc Ponty also made a substantial contribution to bringing the violin into the contemporary jazz arena. Ponty is the son of a violin teacher. Though his early jazz violin inspirations were Grappelli and Smith, Ponty emerged in the mid-Sixties as an intense and impressive improviser with a solo vocabulary that owed as much to the work of John Coltrane as to other violinists – if not

more – though jazz-rock later blunted his edge.

Since Ponty, a considerable number of imposing violinists have come to the fore – some in fusion music (notably American Jerry Goodman and Frenchman Didier Lockwood) and some on the avant-garde (Americans Leroy Jenkins and Billy Bang). Potentially one of the most influential, the Polish musician Zbigniew Seifert died at the age of 33, but he had already recorded extensively, written a 25-minute concerto for violin, orchestra and jazz group, and was a highly regarded guest on European jazz festivals.

In avant-garde violin playing, the most influential practitioner was someone with only a peripheral interest in the instrument – Ornette Coleman. Coleman occasionally used the violin as a solo instrument, principally in a textural manner full of dense, scurrying sounds, percussive attack and skidding, high-pitched dissonance.

A trained player who took this general stratagem

as a catalyst to a new kind of jazz violin voice is Leroy Jenkins. But for all the inspiration of Ornette Coleman to explore new avenues, Jenkins's sound is mostly clear, uncluttered and devoted to the unambiguous presentation of melody, albeit the spiky and angular melodies of the avant-garde.

The example of Jenkins energized the career of the Alabama-born violinist Billy Bang, originally Billy Walker. Bang was trained on violin, but abandoned it for drums and flute in the 1960s, returning to it to form the String Trio of New York in the mid-Seventies, a guitar-bass-violin group that covered jazz, formal music and gypsy styles. Latterly, Billy Bang, whose sound as an improviser resembles a violin version of Ornette Coleman's skewed lyricism, has come to be an increasingly popular guest of orthodox jazz establishments – his music blending the tonality of the post-free-jazz era with the logical structures of more conventional styles.

The Vibes
The vibraphone or vibraharp is a development of the xylophone. Invented around 1920, it features metal

keys attached to vertical hollow tubes, the exits of which can be rapidly opened and closed by rotating fans which produce a vibrato effect.

Lionel Hampton and Red Norvo were the two musicians who first revealed the improvisational possibilities of the vibes in jazz. Hampton, a drummer originally, delivered an extrovert, hard-hitting, riff-inclined style on the instrument, displaying it in both the celebrated Benny Goodman small groups and later with his own barnstorming and sometimes rather flagwaving big band.

Norvo, a white musician who had begun as a xylophone player, possessed a much more subtle and refined style. He is notable for his fast technique (Norvo stoops over the instrument and holds the mallets close to the keyboard), little use of the vibrato, and highly imaginative phrasing. A Norvo trio of the early Fifties featured Charles Mingus as its bass player, and the vibist has long been fond of chamber-like ensembles in which a high degree of melodic interplay is possible. Norvo also demonstrated that, unlike many swing musicians, he was not disconcerted by bebop. Terry Gibbs, a distinctive

LEFT *A violinist equipped for the stormy waters of post 1960s' jazz. Billy Bang has both a quick melodic imagination and an insight into the more abstract approach of sometime violinist Ornette Coleman.*

ABOVE *Red Norvo and Gary Burton – one of the founding fathers of jazz vibes, with one of his virtuosic descendants. Norvo vastly expanded the potential of vibes, and Burton developed their tonal scope.*

vibes soloist with the late Forties Woody Herman band, was similarly inclined.

The Detroit instrumentalist Milt Jackson was next in line. Just as the more recent crop of violinists came under the influence of John Coltrane rather than other violinists. Milt Jackson in the 1940s was influenced by Charlie Parker rather than by Norvo or Hampton. Jackson, who first surfaced in the bebop big band of Dizzy Gillespie, extends the improvised line longer than the earlier vibists. He has a rounded vibrating tone and is an excellent blues player. He builds many of his solos around favourite devices

such as the drum-roll-like hammering of a repeated note, and a characteristic ascending and immediately descending short double-time figure with which he shifts the momentum from the theme statement to the solo. Jackson has appeared with many of the finest musicians of the bebop era, but his best-known setting is the Modern Jazz Quartet, in which he shared the bulk of the solo responsibilities with pianist John Lewis.

But if Milt Jackson sought to adapt the vibes to the bebop idiom, many more recent practitioners have tried to emphasize the special qualities of the instrument as well as absorb the melodic ideas being produced by other improvisers. These have included Gary Burton, Bobby Hutcherson and Walt Dickerson. The latter two have listened to Coltrane; Gary Burton, a musician with many features of lyricism, country influences and coolness in common with pianist Keith Jarrett, has been in the forefront of extending vibes technique. Burton can play complicated chordal pieces with several mallets at once, has a technique for bending notes, and his contemplative and graceful style owes clear allegiances to the pianist

Bill Evans.

Of the most recent vibraphonists, Germans Gunter Hampel and Karl Berger, and American Jay Hoggard have made the most substantial impact.

The Flute

Most jazz flautists – notably James Moody, Rahsaan Roland Kirk, Sam Rivers and Eric Dolphy – were better known as saxophonists. Moody in particular, however, has long been regarded as a musician who has not simply turned to the flute for special effects but who can elicit bebop from it as readily as he can from a saxophone and with none of the unfinished sounding phrasing, weak emphasis or evaporating intonation that blights a good deal of jazz flute playing.

The most commercially successful flute player, Herbie Mann, has always been willing to experiment with influences and idioms that might broaden the appeal of his music – first with ethnic musics from Latin America and the Middle East, then jazz-rock fusion. The knack was so successful that for 13 years he remained top of the *Downbeat* readers poll for flute until a player of superior sound and technique, Hubert Laws, eventually deposed him.

If the principal problem with the flute in the jazz ensemble is the difficulty of making its feathery sound seem anything other than ethereal and insub-

LEFT *Milt Jackson, the bebop vibist par excellence. Usually associated with the Modern Jazz Quartet, Jackson has nevertheless delivered some of his finest solo playing as a leader.*

ABOVE *Bobby Hutcherson, a vibist with a similar melodic imagination to Jackson, but fascinated also by the dense and crowded styles of the 1960s' saxophone avant-garde.*

stantial against the muscular assertiveness of the tenor, or the percussive piano, or the drums, there was always the ingenious unpredictability of some unique improvisers to reconstruct it. In the mid-Fifties the baritone saxist Sahib Shihab was practising a technique of 'overblowing' – singing through the instrument at the same time as blowing it – and the multi-instrumentalist Rahsaan Roland Kirk extended this in the Sixties. Adventurous flautists also began to exploit the attentiveness which the sonority of the flute occasions in the right hands to use even subtler adaptations – notably the sounds made by the pads opening and closing, a fluttering sound like the beating of wings or the running of moccasined feet.

Probably the most influential flautist of the 'free-jazz' era was Eric Dolphy, who revealed a delicate, accessible and romantic side of his musical personality on the instrument that was sometimes difficult to detect in the fierce and explosive variations he would unleash on the other reed instruments – qualities audible in his 'Gazzelloni' on the celebrated album 'Out To Lunch'.

Dolphy's exploration of a freer method of improvisation on flute was taken further by a musician with a fuller, richer tone than him – the classically trained James Newton. And as jazz increasingly forges links with the musical vocabularies of other parts of the world, hybrids of flute vocabulary have surfaced with increasing frequency. The Brazilian musician Hermeto Pascoal – an influence on the 'Bitches Brew'-era Miles Davis – Japanese Hozan Yamamoto and American Lew Tabackin are all taking the potential of the instrument further. In Britain a young black performer, Phillip Bent, is revealing the potential of a rich, 'classical' intonation and a set of musical enthusiasms that bridge jazz, funk and fusion.

GLOSSARY

Axe: Jazz musicians' slang for a musical instrument.

Bebop or *Bop:* Name derived from the sound of vocalists mimicking the phrasing of the music conceived by Charlie Parker, Dizzy Gillespie *et al* in the 1940s. The music was characterized by increased harmonic sophistication (often 'augmenting' the regular chords of standard tunes with extra notes and using these as the basis for improvising), and a frequent shifting of the rhythmic accents from the strong to the weak beats (*offbeats*).

Boogie: Early blues piano style in which right-hand improvisation takes place over a highly rhythmic repeated left-hand bass figure.

Book (usually '*the book*'): A collection of arrangements forming the repertoire of a particular musician or ensemble.

Break: Brief solo statement, usually made unaccompanied during a measured pause by the other members of the band.

Bridge: Short passage linking two parts of the main theme of a tune.

Cakewalk: Early 20th century American dance style.

Chart: Written arrangement of a tune.

Chops: Jazz musicians' parlance for technical facility on an instrument.

Circular breathing: Saxophone technique for taking in breath through the nose and expelling it through the mouthpiece to avoid pauses for breath during playing.

Cool: Musical genre, usually taken to begin in the late Forties and characterized as a quieter, more restrained and sometimes romantic adaptation of bebop.

Counterpoint: The interweaving of simultaneous melody lines.

Cutting ('*cutting contests*'): Competitive manner of soloing – sometimes deliberately and explicitly embarked on, sometimes not – in which a succession of players attempt to outdo each other. Notable feature of after-hours performances by Thirties swing band stars.

Diatonic scale: Basis of most Western art music, a scale of eight notes (do-re-mi etc) consisting of five whole note intervals and two half-notes, the eighth an octave above the first.

Dixieland: Early New Orleans ensemble style; the expression now usually refers to white revivalism of the method.

Four-four: Four beats to the bar, the most frequent rhythmic pattern encountered in jazz, sometimes called 'common time' in general music usage. In the shift from New Orleans music to swing and subsequently bebop the 'accenting' of the beat by drummers shifted from the so-called 'strong beats' (one and three) to the 'weak beats' (two and four).

Gig: Originally a temporary engagement or booking for a jazz musician – might refer to a night's employment, or a longer period in the same venue. Latterly extended by some to include any kind of paid work.

Hard bop: Adaptation of bebop in the 1950s, with a concentration on prolonged solos, considerable use of blues, and frequently a heated, aggressive style.

Harmonics: 'Extra' notes produced by vibrations occurring when a fundamental note is played. Saxophonists of the post-Coltrane era frequently use this device to produce notes beyond the range normally conceived of for the instrument.

Harmony: Two or more notes sounded simultaneously to provide an underpinning for melody. Provides the 'vertical' musical dimension – i.e. describing events happening at one given moment – supporting the 'horizontal' ones of melody, counterpoint and rhythm, which proceed during time.

Horn: Usually a reference to all types of wind instrument, but can refer to any instrument.

Jamming: Improvisation. Often refers to a spontaneous encounter between musicians.

Jive: Insiders' language developed in the jazz world.

Jump: Musical style that predated rock 'n' roll, small group jazz derived from swing but with a strong emphasis on blues and driving rhythm.

Mainstream: The principal course of development of jazz from New Orleans and swing, through bop and free music. New developments are envisaged as happening in reaction to, or feeding into, the mainstream.

Modal playing: Method of improvising over cycles of scales rather than chord progressions – common in early musics and non-European music, notably Indian. Was adopted by Miles Davis from his 'Milestones' and 'Kind of Blue' era onward, and by the later John Coltrane.

New Orleans music: Collective improvising style with the lead taken by the trumpet, and counterpoints provided by clarinet and trombone.

Pentatonic scale: Scale frequently used in folk music, consisting of five notes, spaced a whole tone apart.

Ragtime: Written form of pre-jazz, originally for piano and derived from a mixture of European dance forms and African rhythmic variations. Rhythms are 'syncopated' by accenting the 'strong' beats in one hand and the 'weak' beats in the other.

Riff: Short, repeated musical phrase providing both a rhythmic and a harmonic function behind a soloist. Common feature of swing orchestras.

Scat-singing: Form of wordless singing to imitate the sound of instrumental jazz phrasing. Louis Armstrong is usually taken to be its originator.

Set: Continuous on-stage performance by a musician or band, followed by an interval or the end of the show, viz, 'first set', 'second set' etc.

Sideman: Member of a band other than the leader.

Stride piano: Early jazz piano style, with some ragtime ingredients but featuring improvisation. The left hand plays figures that alternate bass notes with chords in a syncopated manner.

Swing: Two meanings. One refers to the rhythmic character of the jazz beat, a tendency to propel or delay the accenting of the main pulse in a manner that creates anticipation and a sense of momentum, but which is not transcribable in conventional European notation. The other meaning is generic, and refers to the popular style forged in the mid-Thirties, mostly for big-bands and dependent on a smooth, even accenting of the four beats of the bar.

Tailgate: Trombone style deploying long slurs and swooping notes, an expression derived from the need for trombonists to sit over the tailgate of the New Orleans 'bandwagons' so that the slides of their instruments didn't hit their colleagues.

Third stream music: Fusion of contemporary classical chamber music and jazz in the 1950s.

Woodshedding: Jazz musicians' expression for dropping out of public performance to practise or develop some aspect of the art.

Work song: Style of singing developed to replicate the rhythms and momentum of particular types of work. Usually associated with Afro-American slavery.

BIBLIOGRAPHY

Derek Bailey, *Improvisation* (Moorland Publishing, 1980)

Whitney Balliett, *The Sound of Surprise* (Pelican, 1963)

Joachim Berendt, *The Jazz Book* (Granada, 1983)

Stan Britt, *The Jazz Guitarists* (Blandford, 1984)

Brian Case, Stan Britt and Chrissie Murray, *The Illustrated Encyclopedia of Jazz* (Salamander, 1986)

John Chilton, *Sidney Bechet – Wizard of Jazz* (Macmillan, 1987)

James Lincoln Collier, *Duke Ellington* (Michael Joseph, 1987)

James Lincoln Collier, The Making of Jazz (Granada, 1978)

Leonard Feather, *The Encyclopaedia of Jazz in the Seventies* (Quartet, 1976)

Gary Giddings, *Rhythm-a-ning – Jazz Tradition and Innovation in the '80s* (Oxford University Press, 1986)

Gary Giddings, *Riding on a Blue Note – Jazz and American Pop* (Oxford University Press, 1981)

Kitty Grime, *Jazz Voices* (Quartet, 1983)

Ed. Nat Hentoff and Albert McCarthy, *Jazz* (Quartet, 1977)

Andre Hodeir, *Jazz – Its Evolution and Essence* (Grove Press, New York, 1956)

John Litweiler, *The Freedom Principle – Jazz After 1958* (Blandford, 1985)

Francis Newton, *The Jazz Scene* (Penguin, 1961)

Sally Placksin, *Jazzwomen – 1900 to the present* (Pluto, 1982)

Brian Priestley, *Mingus – A Critical Biography* (Quartet, 1982)

Ross Russell, *Bird Lives!* (Quartet, 1972)

Valerie Wilmer, *As Serious As Your Life* (Pluto, 1987)

INDEX